A Child of
Sanitariums

A Child of Sanitariums

*A Memoir of Tuberculosis
Survival and Lifelong Disability*

GLORIA PARIS

McFarland & Company, Inc., Publishers
Jefferson, North Carolina, and London

Library of Congress Cataloguing-in-Publication Data

Paris, Gloria, 1931–
    A child of sanitariums : a memoir of tuberculosis survival and
lifelong disability / Gloria Paris.
        p.   cm.
    Includes bibliographical references and index.

    ISBN: 978-0-7864-5939-1
    softcover : 50# alkaline paper ∞

    1. Paris, Gloria, 1931– — Health.   2. Tuberculosis in
children — United States — Biography.   3. Tuberculosis —
Hospitals — United States.   I. Title.
RC312.6.C4P37   2010
616.9'95 — dc22   2010021733

British Library cataloguing data are available

Front cover: Paris in 1936, at Mercy Hospital

Manufactured in the United States of America

McFarland & Company, Inc., Publishers
    Box 611, Jefferson, North Carolina 28640
    www.mcfarlandpub.com

Dedicated with all my love
to my husband John
and to our children
Stephen, Greg and Anne

Contents

Acknowledgments

This is my story as I remember it. There are events which took place a long time ago that are vivid in my memory, while there are other things during certain periods of my life that I have little or no recollection of. Perhaps these are painful memories that I have unknowingly blocked out of my mind. This book would never have been written if I had not saved all of my journals, and the newspaper articles, pictures, and other memorabilia relating to my life. These things were a tremendous help in recalling and presenting events in chronological order. I am not a professional writer, but writing has always been an important part of my life.

My story is too personal to be told in anyone's words but my own. My original intent was to write a short memoir just for my family. As I began writing I found myself including so much more about tuberculosis, my hospital families, and how my entire life was changed by it. There are several instances in which I have changed names to protect identities. My only regret is that I did not have a chance to talk to so many people who influenced my life but are no longer with us.

It would have been impossible for me to write this book without the help of my incredible family. I wish to express my love and thanks to my husband John. He carefully edited each draft of my manuscript. I am indebted to him for his encouragement and support when I needed it, and his patience and understanding when I spent so much time in my research and writing. He brought our family on many of what they called mom's annual pilgrimages to the sanitarium which had been my home for years. John made many additional journeys with me, pushing my wheelchair through both sanitariums that were now either vacant or being used to house other facilities. There I took notes and reminisced, gathering material for this book. He encouraged me to continue writing when painful memories emerged and I did not want to go on with it.

Thanks to our remarkable children — Anne, Greg, and Steve — who have always given me so much love and have made my life so enjoyable. I love them very much and am indebted to them for their support and help in making this book possible. Steve, our oldest, was of immense help in gathering family history along with his wife, Wendy. Greg gave me my first computer and printer and taught me how to use them. He helped me with the many problems I encountered in learning how to use them. A book he gave me about writing memoirs was a wonderful guide. Anne spent hours carefully reviewing each chapter and offering suggestions. When my laptop finally gave out in the middle of writing this book she presented me with a new one. Special thanks to my son-in-law, Joe Orsene, whose expertise and assistance with countless internet problems and the final organization of the book for submission is deeply appreciated. Our young grandsons— Kyle, Brandon, Giovanni, Sebastian, and Luciano— motivated me with their constant "Is the book done yet, Nane? When can we read it?"

My parents, Anne and Alexander Didio, passed away before I started this incredible journey into my past. I wish these two remarkable people were still with us. They had rarely talked about my tuberculosis. However, just before my father passed away he began sharing with me the memories of my long illness and their constant struggle to cope with it. I am deeply grateful to my sister Maryann (Stevers) Prosser and aunts Mary (Tony) Ciao, Elsie (Frank) Didio-LeGravanese, and great-aunt Delia (Arthur) Giovannini for allowing me to interview them. They all graciously filled me in with much of our family history, ethnic heritage, and the customs and traditions of Italian Americans. I was able to trace the Giovannini family history thanks to the outstanding job my cousin Maria (Giovannini) McGraw did in putting it all together for everyone. Thank you to my dear Uncle Aldo, who left us all too early in life, for saving some of my letters and sharing their contents with me years later.

I have no contact with those who made up my various hospital families. I am sure that most of them, as well as many of the relatives and friends who are mentioned in this book, are no longer with us. To all of them I will always be grateful for sharing with me their stories, many of which I had recorded in my journals, never realizing how important they would be in writing this book. They affected my life in extraordinary ways.

To my dear lifelong friends from the class of 1949 who were so kind and helpful in helping me recall much of what I had forgotten in our years at Mynderse Academy — I thank you all. They are Angie Bantivantus, Julie (Mellini) Cracknell, Netta (Lilla) DeJohn, Gloria (Marciano) Dragone, Delores (Johnson) Leone, Jean (Suglia) Osso, and Barbara (Yates) Rizzieri, as well as the entire class of 1949. I have fond memories of their compassion and support as I attended my first "real" school.

My fellow members of the Finger Lakes Writer's Group gave me invaluable suggestions as they critiqued my book chapter by chapter. I am so grateful to all of them for encouraging me to seek publication. A special thanks to members retired teacher Ellen Clark, who edited my first draft, and Richard Ciciarelli, author and former English teacher, who guided me through language and grammar skills.

Two people who helped me tremendously in my research of the hospitals were Sister Linda Ann Palmisano, administrator of Mercy Health & Rehabilitation Center in Auburn New York, and Julie Carney, an alderman of the city of Oneonta, New York, Julie invited John and me to Oneonta, where she took us on a memorable tour of the main and children's buildings of Homer Folks. Staff members there gave us information about the buildings and made copies of pictures of them for us. I was given a copy of Elaine M. Wadleigh's booklet *A Study in the Changing Functions of Homer Folks.* Dr. Stanley N. Lincoln, former director of Biggs while I was a patient there, granted me permission to use the huge volumes containing my medical records for my college thesis, "Tuberculosis of the Bones and Joint." Volunteers and staff of the DeWitt Historical Society in Ithaca assisted me in my research of Biggs, and gave me access to the Biggs Hospital Collection, which included articles written by staff doctors about tuberculosis from both a clinical and a psychological view, as well as Ithaca newspaper articles regarding Biggs.

A special thanks to Guy T. Cosentino, former executive director of Options for Independence (OFI), and my fellow members of the board who presented me with books and tapes about writing. Thank you, senator Michael F. Nozzolio, for permission to include a reference to the award you presented to me on behalf of the New York State Senate. Jim Bero, your story was incredible. Thanks for the interview. Thank you, Sal Traina, for sharing with me your experiences in writing and for presenting me with my first copy of the *Writer's Market.* Walter Gable, Seneca County historian, did an outstanding job in the local marketing of my book.

Prologue

Today someone in the world is newly infected with the tuberculosis bacilli (germ) every second. Tuberculosis is an airborne infectious disease that has existed for thousands of years and refuses to go away. Today it remains a major international problem, and the complacent feeling that it has been totally eradicated is false. After several decades of optimism and steadily declining cases there has been a resurgence of this devastating and often fatal disease. More people have tuberculosis today than any other time in history. According to the World Health Organization (WHO) it is a global health emergency. It is the number one killer among infectious diseases in the world. Approximately two billion people (one-third of the world's population) are believed to be infected with the pathogenic bacillus. Most of these people live in the developing countries of Africa, Asia and Latin America. In the United States an estimated ten million persons are presently infected with *Mycobacterium tuberculosis*, the bacteria that are the cause of this disease.

* * *

In the 1930s, at the age of five, I was a victim of tuberculosis of the bones and joints. There was no cure. At that time it took more lives than any other disease, and its greatest toll was in young people. Many children died. I spent the next nine years confined in sanitariums. This was followed by another five years of continued monitoring and several surgeries. Once discharged, adjustment to the outside world was difficult. People pitied me, stared at me, and treated me differently. For the first

1

time in my life, I now felt different. Although I became a survivor, the effects of this disease changed my entire life.

Tuberculosis is a common and often deadly bacterial infectious disease caused by *Mycobacterium tuberculosis*. Although it usually attacks the lungs, it can also affect other parts of the body such as the brain, kidney, spinal fluid, bones and joints. When it settles in the lungs it is called pulmonary, and when it appears elsewhere it is called extra-pulmonary. What is important to know is that there is a difference in being infected with tuberculosis (latent) and actually having the disease (active). Those who are infected have the bacteria in their body, but the body's defenses protect them and they are not sick. In the active disease people are sick and can spread the disease to others.

Bovine tuberculosis is transmitted from animals to humans and vice versa. It was widespread when I was a child. Children are great consumers of milk, and drinking raw contaminated (unpasteurized) milk containing the bovine bacillus was a source of infection. Most people were not aware of the danger posed by the very milk they drank or gave to their children. By the time programs for testing cattle and destroying infected animals, along with pasteurization of milk, were mandated, children all over the world had become victims of bovine tuberculosis. They spent years in sanitariums, often suffering from the many serious complications of this devastating disease. Some did not survive.

Tuberculosis of the bone usually does not occur unless there is tuberculosis somewhere else in the body. Bacilli travel from the blood or lymph nodes to bony terminals and lodge there, multiply, and the tuberculosis disease process begins. These bacilli may also spread into the joints, where tubercles (lesions) are formed that may come together (coalesce) and cause softening. Frequent abscesses may form, destroying a large amount of bone. This can lead to dislocation and growth disturbances.

There are three strains of organisms that cause tuberculosis— *Mycobacterium tuberculosis*, *Mycobacterium bovis*, and *Mycobacterium africanum*. It was the progressive assault of the bovis strain on my young body that resulted in my type of tuberculosis.

Even if a person had the characteristic signs of this disease, tuberculosis in these areas was difficult to diagnosis, and even more difficult to treat. There was no cure. I am amazed that somehow I was able to survive this devastating disease.

* * *

When I started gathering information for this memoir it was with the intent that it would be written just for my family — my husband, our children and our grandchildren. Up until that time I had rarely talked to them about my unusual childhood, my disease, and the disability that resulted from it. I was concerned that they would be upset once they found out what had happened to me. Perhaps our children would worry that the same thing could happen to them or to their children.

It was not until I had retired and my children were grown that I decided to share my story with them. Writing it brought back to the surface long-forgotten memories. Some were pleasant and often humorous, while others were not. There were times when I felt I just could not go on. There has not been a single day that I have not thought about this, often going over parts of my life over and over again in my mind. That is why I have been able to write, often in great detail, events that happened so long ago.

In writing this memoir I soon became completely absorbed not only with my story, but with learning more about the disease itself, how the public reacted to it, the sanitarium cure, how those afflicted coped with it, the role of the federal and state governments in its control and prevention, and the movement for disability rights. My story would not be complete if I did not include my incredible hospital family. They were young adults, most of whom had tuberculosis of the lung.

As one of over forty million disabled people in the United States, I have come to terms with my disability and with the events that changed my life. I have learned that it is okay to be disabled, that it is not necessary to be in denial or to pretend that the disability does not exist. From the day we are born things that happen to us affect our lives.

People with disabilities have finally come out of the closet and have led a successful disability rights movement. Along with the passage of the Americans with Disabilities Act (ADA) in 1990 they have become more independent, proving that they can lead useful and productive lives.

Today, following the decline and resurgence of tuberculosis, a more health-conscious and informed public is expressing a great deal of interest in tuberculosis. There is hope that eventually this devastating disease will be permanently eliminated.

"*The woman who survives intact and happy must be at once tender and tough. She must have convinced herself, or be in the unending process of convincing herself, that she, her values, and her choices are important.*"

— Maya Angelou
*Wouldn't Take Nothing
for My Journey Now*

Mercy Hospital

At the age of five I climbed on a chair to reach for my favorite doll. It was a beautiful doll with long blond hair, a pink bonnet and matching coat. She had been placed on top of the high dresser in my room. Since I could not reach my doll, I pulled a chair over to the dresser and climbed on it. As the chair slid from under me, I lost my balance and fell. This fall aggravated an undetected disease that had been silently invading my young body for some time. From that moment on my life would be changed forever.

Following the fall, I experienced severe recurrent pain in my left leg. The pain only subsided when I was either sitting or lying down. When I tried to walk, I often lost my balance and fell. Soon my falling down became a serious problem. As I unconsciously tried not to put as much weight on this leg I developed a pronounced limp. During the weeks that followed my general health began to fail. Every day I ran a low-grade fever. Since I had no appetite, and nothing my mother prepared appealed to me, I gradually began to lose weight. Every day I grew weaker.

My mother was distraught and unable to hide her fears as she asked my father what he thought was wrong with me. He was as concerned as she was, but tried to hide his own anxious feelings. In order to console her he tried to convince her that it was probably nothing serious. Together they spent sleepless nights with their constant worry about my condition. Like so many parents of children who become ill, they were in denial. Relatives and friends that they talked to about it assured them that whatever it was, it would simply improve with time. When it did not, and my condition deteriorated even more, they became frantic.

Left: In my parents' backyard during the summer of 1934, two years before the fall. *Right:* In 1934 I was a healthy, active child. I loved playing with my two uncles, Victor and David Giovannini, my mother's youngest brothers.

Prior to the fall I had been a very active child. My father enjoyed telling people about the time he brought me to the movies and one of the ushers asked us to leave because I was running up and down the aisle. How I loved to run, and when my father and I went for walks and to the park we ran together. Sometimes we would race, and occasionally he purposely slowed down so that I was the winner. Then he would pick me up and twirl me around, laughing and shouting my name, as he told anyone within hearing distance that I was indeed the fastest runner ever.

He thoroughly enjoyed his memory of me as a little girl, healthy and strong, running and jumping. This was a memory of our special times together, times that he now feared might never happen again. Things were so different now as I had to be kept still in order to alleviate the pain.

Although everything was done to make me comfortable, I was restless and longed to be up and around. My mother encouraged me to remain in bed. She would sit on my bed, put her arms around me, and tell me that she wanted me to stay in bed so that I would get well and be able to run and play again. My parents placed toys on my bed and spent hours playing with me. Sometimes they would lie on the bed and read to me, or just hold me and tell me how much they loved me. There were nights that I cried out in pain, a result of muscle spasms. Sometimes when I woke up I would find one of my parents still lying there beside me.

On days that I felt better I was allowed to play outside for a short period of time. Several weeks after my fall, while playing outside with one of my cousins, I again lost my balance and fell. This time, however, I began screaming in pain. Nothing my parents did seemed to ease the agonizing pain. My father gently picked me up, carried me into the house, and laid me on my bed. He looked at my mother. She was crying. They both knew that nothing that they were doing seemed to help. It was time to take me to the doctor. Since they did not even have the five dollars they needed to take me to their family doctor, they simply did not know what to do.

Devout Catholics, they had relied on their faith in God and their own parenting to bring about my recovery. Like millions of Americans caught in the midst of the Great Depression, they barely had enough money for food and the rent for our sparsely furnished apartment. My father was unemployed. There was no money for medical care. When one of my aunts came to see how I was doing and heard about their plight, she insisted on giving them the five dollars needed for an office visit. They assured her that they would pay her back as soon as they could. Her financial situation was not much better than theirs, but she wanted desperately to help.

We did not even own a car, but my aunt insisted on driving us to the office of our family doctor, Dr. DeMarco. When we arrived at the office my parents were very worried about what the doctor would tell them. Dr. DeMarco lifted me up on his examination table. As he examined me it was obvious that he was very upset. He asked them why they waited so long to bring me to see him. They were too embarrassed to tell him why they had not brought me in sooner.

After a thorough examination he explained the seriousness of my condition to them. They were very frightened and feared the worst. Dr. DeMarco looked at them solemnly as he explained to them that my poor health, along with my symptoms of weakness, weight loss, low-grade fever, and intense pain on falling, was of real concern to him. Because of my joint and muscle pain he thought that I might possibly have rheumatism. Rheumatism was the name given to any disorder of muscles, tendons, bones and joints. It is characterized by pain, discomfort and disability.

Dr. DeMarco ordered serial x-rays of my left leg. After this visit a follow-up appointment was made. By then he would have the results of my x-rays and could possibly make a diagnosis.

Although the first x-ray image was recorded just before the beginning of the twentieth century, it was not until the 1930s that clearer images resulted in their importance as a medical diagnostic tool. Still it was not until the 1950s that even better imaging made it easier for doctors to make an accurate diagnosis.

When we returned home to our tiny apartment, I could sense that something was very wrong. My parents seemed very somber and talked in hushed tones. They felt guilty about waiting so long to get medical attention for me and were worried about what would happen next. When they told their parents about what had happened they were assured that they would help them out with the care I would now need.

On my follow-up visit Dr. DeMarco had the results of the x-rays. He explained to my parents that I had to be hospitalized immediately. He was still not sure what was causing my symptoms. The next step would be to obtain a more thorough medical evaluation and to have me on complete bed rest until he could figure out what was going on.

This was just a month before my sixth birthday. I had been in kindergarten for just three weeks. My parents were emotionally drained, and my mother seemed unusually quiet as she packed some of my clothes and favorite dolls. They still did not have a car, so my father's parents drove us to Mercy Hospital, a Catholic hospital located in the small city of Auburn in upstate New York where we lived. A receptionist at the front desk filled in my admission forms. Then a nun who was also a nurse came in, wheeling a strange-looking wooden chair. It had a very large wheel on each side. She was dressed just like the nuns at school, except she wore white instead of black.

"Are you Gloria?" she asked.

"Yes I am," I replied, pleased that she knew my name.

She picked me up and asked if I would like to sit in this chair and go for a little ride. When I agreed she put me down in this odd looking chair. She explained that it was called a wheelchair because it was a chair that had wheels. Somehow she thought that was funny, but I was too worried about where she was taking me to appreciate her humor. This chair

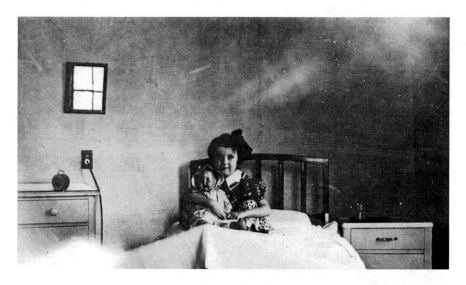

This is my room at Mercy Hospital, where I would remain for about one year.

with wheels was very uncomfortable, even when this nurse raised the two leg rests and placed my legs on them. She wheeled me down several long corridors while my parents followed. I kept looking back to make sure they were still there. We passed many rooms where I saw people lying in bed. It was very quiet here. Finally I was wheeled into a small room that looked something like my bedroom at home, except the bed was very high. It was a plain-looking room, and the white bedspread and curtains were not as pretty as the ones at home that my mother had made for me. A container for water and a glass were the only things on the dark brown nightstand next to the bed. There was nothing else in the room.

After I was lifted into the bed and placed under the covers by the nurse who had wheeled me to the room, she told me her name was Sister Mary Margaret. She explained that this was the room where I would be staying. *What did she mean?* I thought to myself. *Won't I be going home tomorrow?*

When my parents started to leave I asked them if they could spend the night with me. My mother explained that they were not allowed to, but told me that they would be back the first thing in the morning.

I was confused. *Why was I here?*

I was frightened. *What was going to happen next?*

I was alone. *Why had my parents abandoned me?*

*   *   *

Mercy Hospital was originally established in 1919 through the efforts of the Reverend William Payne, former pastor of St. Mary's Church in Auburn. This was the church that my parents attended and where I had been baptized. Originally this hospital had consisted of two frame buildings with a capacity of merely 20 beds. In the year I was born a new hospital was erected with a bed capacity of 104.

I occupied one of the beds in this hospital for nearly a year. The Reverend Payne had obtained the support and assistance of the Sisters of Saint Francis from the nearby city of Syracuse. Mercy Hospital provided medical aid and hospital care to everyone, regardless of race, religion, or economic status. My parents did not have to worry about how they would pay for my care there. No one was ever turned away.

Sister Mary Margaret, my favorite nun, finds me napping in my chair.

Up until the time I was admitted the only nuns I had ever seen were the teachers at the Catholic school I had attended briefly. They had all worn black and looked quite stern. Here most of the nurses were nuns. Their uniforms consisted of a floor-length white habit along with a large stiff white collar and a veil. They all lived in a nearby convent where they obeyed the three vows of poverty, chastity and obedience.

At night the nuns took turns reading me bedtime stories and teaching me simple evening prayers. Sometimes they sang to me until I fell asleep. How I loved these dedicated and caring women. My favorite nun, Sister Mary Margaret, seemed younger than all the rest. She was always laughing and sometimes made faces behind the other nuns and mimicked them. I had become such a serious little girl, bewildered by my new surroundings and upset every time my parents had to leave. Once she said to me, "You are like a little sister to me. Let's pretend we are really sisters, but we won't tell the others."

From then on Sister Mary Margaret became my only playmate, as well as my older sister.

* * *

Even though he did not yet have a diagnosis, Dr. DeMarco was still convinced that I had either rheumatism or what was often referred to as growing pains. He felt that with bed rest and a proper diet I would eventually gain strength and get well.

Dr. DeMarco was very optimistic when he talked to my parents. He told them that I would no doubt be one of the lucky ones who would heal quickly, simply letting nature take its course. Perhaps he felt that there was no purpose in telling them anything more. They were already resigned to the fact that I would be a patient at Mercy for a very long time.

In order to alleviate the severe and persistent pain I suffered, a pulley device called traction was applied to my leg. Traction is often used in an effort to overcome deformity by helping to return the joint to its original position, thus reducing pain. Both sides of my leg were supported by a thick canvas material which went underneath my foot and was held in place by wide straps. Sand bags were then placed on each side of my leg to keep it immobile. Next a pulley was attached to the canvas and to the ropes which were then hung over the end of my bed. A pouch was attached to the end of these ropes and was used to hold weights. These weights could be easily changed, adding more or less weight according to the doctor's assessment of the traction. Now my leg was fairly well immobilized and stretched.

Although my parents were afraid that this course of treatment would be very painful, the opposite was true. Once my leg was placed in traction and weights were applied, the pain was greatly reduced. Still it was very confining since I was unable to either turn over or turn on either side. Now I was not able to leave my bed — the once active child was now completely inactive.

One day several of the nuns heard me screaming and ran down the hall to see what was wrong. Nothing they did or said could quiet me, and they could not figure out why I was in such distress. As I lay there in agonizing pain, they discovered that someone had mistakenly removed the weights from the traction pouch. Minutes after the weights were replaced the pain subsided.

*   *   *

It was not long after the incident with the weights that a diagnosis was finally made. Dr. DeMarco told my parents that I had skeletal tuberculosis involving both my hip and joint. This diagnosis was based on my latest series of x-rays as well as my case history. There was evidence of all of the classic symptoms of this type of tuberculosis. This included the spontaneous pain that occurred after my falls, pain on motion and muscle spasms. I had a low-grade fever and weight loss. Unfortunately my diagnosis and intervention came much too late. In cases like mine, when the patient is in poor health and has low resistance, the damage tends to be much worse. It results in destruction of the bone. Fluid collects and inflames the lining of the joint. The pain, swelling and stiffness had brought about my falling and limping.

Once my parents were over the initial shock of this devastating diagnosis they wanted to know more about the disease. They had heard stories of people who had tuberculosis in their lungs, who were placed in sanitariums for long periods, and who often died.

Dr. DeMarco could see the anxious look on their faces and knew how frightened and alarmed they were. He tried to answer their many questions in terms they could understand without causing them to worry unnecessarily. He explained that there were many different kinds of tuberculosis and that the type that I had was largely a disease of children, especially those who, like me, were in poor health. These children traditionally have little resistance to this disease. It occurs most frequently in the spine and hip, and mine was just in the hip. It was called bovine tuberculosis. There was some good news. My lungs were clear, which meant that I did not have the highly contagious form of the disease.

My parents wanted to know more. They needed to know what was going to happen to me and how I got this disease. My disease, the doctor told them carefully, was caused by tiny (microscopic) organisms called bacteria. These bacteria had traveled through my lymph channels and blood stream to the ends of my bones and joints. There they multiplied rapidly, invading the bone and causing the bones to become soft, erosive and weak. When I fell the impact caused even more destruction and pain.

It still was not clear to my parents what was needed in order for me to get well, return home, and lead a normal life. Was there anything they could do for me? Dr. DeMarco realized that there was nothing he could tell them that would ease their fears. Right now, he explained, the best thing you can do is visit her every day and try to make her life as normal as possible. In time he was sure that I would have a complete recovery, and that I would be able to return home and once again attend school. They were never told that there was no known cure. He also did not tell them about the many complications of bone tuberculosis, or that it can be traced to drinking infected milk. They would learn about all of this soon enough.

Just a few days after they were told about the diagnosis, one of their friends who was visiting confided in them that he had heard that drinking contaminated milk was the cause of my type of tuberculosis. Because this disease mainly affected children, he was convinced that it was the reason I was so sick. My parents became very angry when he told them this. They refused to believe that they had unknowingly given me milk that was spoiled. Still they could not hide their feelings of guilt knowing that, despite the fact that they had fresh milk delivered every day, it was possible that they had unintentionally given me contaminated milk.

They began to wonder why the doctor had not told them this, and they confronted him with it the very next day. They wanted to know why he had not told them about spoiled milk being the cause of bone tuberculosis, and to tell him that they would never have given me milk that was not safe. Dr. DeMarco said he knew that, and that was why he had not said anything. He said he wanted them to understand that it was not their fault and that some milk contains the bacteria from infected cattle. They would have no way of knowing that. It was a major problem and hopefully in time it would be resolved. This time he told them there was no known cure for my type of tuberculosis, but he was still confident that eventually I would have a complete recovery. My parents were satisfied with his explanation, but still felt that somehow they had not taken proper care of me.

* * *

Even though my parents were allowed to visit me every day and stay as long as they wanted, they were very unhappy. It was always harder for them. Their life was difficult enough with the constant stress of living in poverty. Added to this was my frightening situation that no one, including the doctors, could predict the outcome of.

Alone with my dolls on a small balcony at Mercy Hospital in Auburn, New York, in 1936.

Our family had a wonderful support system. Both of my parents came from very large families. I was the first grandchild for both sets of grandparents, and they were overjoyed when I was born. When I became ill they were distraught and, like my parents, did not understand what was going on. My father's family all lived right in Auburn and his parents, brothers, and sisters visited me frequently. Although my mother's family lived about fifteen miles away in the village of Seneca Falls, somehow they managed to visit me several times a week. Even the close friends of my parents came to visit. They were all like family to me.

Everyone did everything they could think of for me, and they all were constantly bringing me candy and other treats so that I would gain weight. My grandfather Massimo brought me Hershey's chocolate bars every time he came. He always hid them in his coat pocket, pretending he had forgotten to bring them. Then he would pull them out slowly and in his heavy Italian accent say, "You thought I forgot didn't you? Grandpa never forgets his favorite little girl."

In place of my drab white bedspread, one of my aunts had made a lovely colorful afghan for my bed. My room was soon filled with books and dolls. These dolls were my imaginary family that helped me through the times when I was alone. It was not long before I became accustomed to the hospital environment. Memories of home, of school, and of playgrounds and playmates gradually vanished.

By summer my general health had improved, although there were still few changes in my x-rays. Now the traction was removed for short periods of time and I was able to leave my bed. There was a tiny balcony near my room. When the weather was warm the nuns would carry me out there and place me in a small armchair along with some of my dolls. They were my only companions and I never tired of them. To me they seemed almost real. One of the dolls was dressed like a nun, and I named her Sister Mary Margaret. It was wonderful to be out of my room and in the fresh air. Even though I sat there with only my dolls for company, I was quite content.

There was a wonderful sweet smell in the air and I wondered what it was. When I asked the sisters they explained that it came from the small lilac trees and shrubs on the hospital grounds below. Even though this balcony was several stories up, I can still remember that sweet fragrance — so unlike the hospital odors I had become accustomed to. Soon my parents were given permission to take me down to the hospital grounds in a wheelchair. There

My parents, Alex and Anne Didio, on one of their daily visits in 1936. They still did not have a diagnosis of my illness.

I finally saw the exquisite purple and white flowers. Now, whenever I am around lilacs, I close my eyes, picture a little girl on a balcony alone and smiling, surrounded by her family of dolls, as the scent of lilacs filled the air.

My parents seemed so much happier now. They were sure that I was on the road to complete recovery and that soon they would be able to take me home. Their happiness, however, was short lived. Dr. DeMarco had to tell them that, despite the fact that I was gaining weight and seemed to be doing so much better, I would not be going back home. Recent serial x-rays confirmed the fact that my tuberculosis was continuing to spread. Even the traction that I had endured for almost a year had not stopped the rapid progression of the disease. Millions more of those microscopic warriors had continue to invade and destroy my hip. There seemed to be no way to stop them.

It had been convenient for my family to have me in a facility near them, so they were completely taken by surprise one day when Dr. DeMarco told them that I definitely needed more care than Mercy Hospital could provide. It was in my best interest, he felt, for me to be admitted to a tuberculosis sanitarium as soon as arrangements could be made.

Sanitariums were being built all over the country, but in the state of New York there were none close to where we lived. Although my parents agonized over this decision, they knew that they really had no choice but to follow the doctor's advice. Plans were made to transfer me to one of these institutions where they specialized in the treatment of all types of tuberculosis.

My parents were told that I would be housed in a separate building for children. There I would be placed under the care of bone specialists, orthopedic doctors, and would receive the best care available. I would be able to attend school and have other children to play with.

Once they agreed to this, plans were immediately made for my transfer. It was to be to the children's building at Homer Folks Memorial Hospital in Oneonta, New York. This hospital was more than one hundred miles from my home.

Within days I was discharged from Mercy. My family of dolls, which had increased in number, and collection of books were packed along with my other belongings. When the nuns and doctors hugged me and said good-bye, I did not really grasp the fact that I would never see them again.

After my diagnosis of tuberculosis in 1936 I am enjoying the lilacs while waiting to be transferred to another hospital.

My experiences during the year I spent at Mercy Hospital are ones that I have gone over again and again in my mind. Somehow I retained in vivid detail this frightening first hospital admission. Eventually these memories faded away. However later on when I was a young woman I started wondering about what had happened to me that had changed my life so dramatically. That is when I began to ask my parents and several relatives about it. Little by little dimmed memories evolved, often in great detail.

Sister Mary Margaret was the last to say goodbye. She held me close and placed a small vase with purple lilacs in it in my hand. Then she leaned over and whispered in my ear, "Goodbye, little sister, I will miss you. Promise me that when you are well you will come back and visit me."

That never happened. I never saw her again.

Homer Folks Hospital

On the day of my transfer the trip was unbearably long. After more than three hours on the road, we finally reached Oneonta. This beautiful city, located high on a hillside overlooking the Susquehanna valley in the foothills of the Catskill Mountains, is called the City of the Hills. It did not take us long to find the buildings of the Homer Folks Tuberculosis Hospital which were spread out over the hills of the campus.

One year before I was born Franklin D. Roosevelt, as governor of New York, submitted a plan to the state legislature recommending the building of more tuberculosis hospitals. He appointed a special commission to investigate health conditions throughout the state. He felt there was a need in those counties which had inadequate or no facilities to take care of people with tuberculosis. As a result of these findings, funds were appropriated for the construction of three sanitariums to serve the needs of 25 rural counties.

Oneonta was chosen as one of the sites in the state for a sanitarium. When the hospital opened in 1935 it was named after Homer Folks, a man well known for his outstanding work in the fields of welfare and public health.

As we entered the beautifully landscaped grounds of the sanitarium, my parents looked on in amazement. They had never realized that it would be anything like this. There were eleven brick buildings, all were different sizes but had the same architectural features. They were spread out on different levels of the steep hills. Majestic trees surrounded the more than two hundred acres of land. A variety of bushes and

At the Homer Folks Tuberculosis Sanitarium children's building in 1937 we spent a lot of time on the long porches.

colorful annual and perennial flowers around each of the buildings and along the sidewalks added to the grandeur of the complex.

Homer Folks was self contained and could accommodate up to 250 patients. There were residences for doctors and nurses, a pharmacy, a laboratory, a post office, store, bakery, library, and a school for the children. Many of the buildings were connected by tunnels leading to the laundry area. Soiled linens which were thought to be infectious were brought there and burned in incinerators.

We drove past the huge main building that we were told was where all of the adult patients were housed. From there we drove up a rather steep hill which led to the children's building. This smaller building overlooked the campus below. Picturesque concrete statues of jungle animals stood guard on each side of the front entrance. This time I was not as frightened as I had been on my first admission. This would be my new home, a home where I would not be the only child but would be living with other children. I was so excited and could not wait to meet them. It was 1937 and later we found out that I was one of the first patients admitted there. I was six years old.

My father carried me into the building where we were met by a young man, an orderly, who escorted us to the admissions office. This time, instead of a wheelchair, the orderly took me from my father's arms and placed me on a stretcher. It was like a small bed on wheels. My parents walked behind as I was wheeled into an elevator. I had never been on an elevator before and thought it was quite exciting, but as the doors closed I found myself suddenly anxious, wondering where I was being taken.

When we reached the second floor and got off the elevator my parents seemed unusually quiet as they walked beside the stretcher. We were taken to a small private room located at the end of a corridor where we were greeted by a nurse. She wore a white uniform and had a funny-looking white cap on her head. She told us that nurses wore caps that signified what nursing school they had graduated from.

"But I thought Gloria would be in a room with other children," my mother said. It was the hospital's policy, the nurse explained, to keep new patients isolated until they have been thoroughly examined. Tests would be taken to see if the disease had spread to any other areas of my body. For now I would remain in a private room.

My mother reluctantly unpacked and arranged my things. She placed my favorite doll, Dopey, next to me. When it was time for them to leave they told me that they would be back to see me in a few days. I had still not grasped the fact that I was now a long distance from home and they would not be coming every day. Their everyday visits were now simply out of the question.

My father tried to hide how troubled he was as he again explained that it would take them many hours to travel from where they lived to Homer Folks. He assured me that they would come to visit me every Sunday, and that they would send me a surprise package to open during the week. His explanation seemed to satisfy me, but when they left my room to return home I felt frightened in this strange new place — and once again abandoned.

As soon as one of the nurses turned off the light in my room and closed my door for the night, I began to worry about what was happening to me.

Where were the good sisters?

Would my parents really come on Sunday?

Where were the other children?

In the stillness of the night, I heard a nurse's footsteps as she went from room to room closing doors. *Were there other children in those rooms?* I began to cry, but no one came to my room to see what was wrong. Perhaps no one heard me. Perhaps the people who worked here did not know how to cope with their sad young patients—children like me who had been taken from their homes and families. We all faced the night alone.

At least I had Dopey — the lovable dwarf in Snow White. Unlike Disney's shy childlike character who never spoke, my Dopey could talk. When I pulled the cord in his back his mouth opened and closed — and he spoke only to me. I was his Snow White.

Dopey had a happy face, protruding ears, and wore a soft pale blue robe with a matching stocking hat and black boots. All were removable, and my mother had made many outfits for him. My favorite was the bright red and white polka dot nightgown that matched the one she made for me. We were quite a handsome pair.

On that first night, feeling completely neglected with only Dopey at my side, I reached down and pulled my covers over my head. Now I could make the real world disappear. I hated this new world. Then I hugged my little friend as I closed my eyes and escaped into an imaginary world. In this world, I left my bed, flew out of the window, and sailed over housetops below. Sometimes I entered homes where the happy children lived. I had never heard of Peter Pan, but I was certainly one of the lost children. Along with my new friends I ran and played until I fell asleep — with Dopey smiling at my side.

In the morning someone opened my door. Since my room was at the very end of the corridor there was very little traffic going by, making me feel even more isolated. Occasionally a nurse or other staff member came into my room, but other than that I saw no one. Most of the nurses were kind enough, but they could not replace the nuns at Mercy who had cared for me so lovingly. These dedicated women had read me bedtime stories and had given me goodnight hugs. There was never any of that in this strange desolate place.

Soon I heard strange sounds and people shouting from below my window. A nurse wheeled my bed close to the window so that I could see what was going on. On the grounds below a group of men were working. When they spotted me they waved.

"What are you doing?" I yelled down, glad to finally have someone to talk to.

They told me they were putting in a swimming pool and that when they were finished I would be able to come down and swim. Every day as I watched them work they would stop to wave and talk to me.

One of the workers shouted up to me one day. "You look just like a little princess in a castle."

Although I sure didn't feel like a princess, and this place was certainly not a castle, his words cheered me up. From that day on the workers called me princess. When I was moved to another section of the hospital I forgot about the pool — which would have been impossible for me to use anyway. It was a long time before anyone called me princess again.

*   *   *

Regaining our health was vital if we were to recover from our illness. One of the general measures necessary for this was proper nutrition. We were given a well-balanced diet that included foods with a high vitamin content. Because I had little or no appetite and either could or would not eat, the staff became very concerned about my recovery. They seemed more concerned about this than about the fact that I was so unhappy. Certainly this was a contributing factor in my inability to eat. My tray would be left on my stand for hours in the hope that I would eat something. No matter how they tried to get me to try something I refused.

Other measures that were essential for our well-being included bed rest. When I was placed in traction I was in bed all of the time. After it was removed there were still long mandatory rest periods, and bedtime was very early.

Fresh air was also important. It had already been established that patients with bovine tuberculosis seemed to do better when exposed to the outdoors whenever possible. Exposing the body to the sun's rays (heliotherapy) was recommended. This was at a time when there were no precautions to exposure to the sun's rays, and I remembered getting sunburn quite often. Still I loved being outdoors and in the sun. In the winter we were taken to a room in the radiology section of the diagnostic area where we were exposed to ultraviolet heating lamps. These were supposed to provide rays similar to those of the sun. It was not the same as being in the real sun, and I dreaded going there.

Local measures included putting the affected part at rest with a splint, brace, traction, or cast. Surgery for bone tuberculosis was often performed in an effort to put the diseased area at complete rest and to hasten recovery. However children usually did not have early surgery because of the importance of preserving motion and the length of the extremity.

Weeks later the doctors at Homer Folks reviewed my condition with my parents. Physical and radiological studies confirmed the diagnosis made at Mercy — I definitely had tuberculosis of the bone and joint. Doctors agreed that it had been transmitted to me through unpasteurized milk from infected cattle. All of the problems that had resulted from my frequent falls were a result of this transmission.

My general condition at that time was fair. Sometimes I still ran a low-grade fever and had an elevated pulse rate. Iron supplements were given to me in an effort to treat the secondary anemia that I had developed. Once again, more traction was applied in yet another attempt to overcome flexion deformity. Periodic x-rays and laboratory tests continued to rule out my having pulmonary tuberculosis. I dreaded it when I was presented with a small cup and was asked to try to cough in order to bring up sputum. All they ever got from me was spit. Actually, that was a good sign that my lungs were clear. One-third of patients with bone and joint tuberculosis have a history of pulmonary disease. It can coexist with the extra-pulmonary form. Still there was the constant worry that I would develop tuberculosis in my lungs.

After several months of making the weekly trip to see me, my parents decided to make a special trip during the week to talk to one of the doctors taking care of me. They wanted to know how long I would be there. A pediatrician who specialized in treating tuberculosis in children set aside time to talk to them. He was used to talking to worried parents and often had to tell them things that were very upsetting. Again my parents feared the worst. They remained silent as he explained to them that my disease was quite extensive, and that he was not sure how long my recovery would take. It could take months, or even years. Nothing he said after that mattered, and they were resigned to the fact that my struggle would go on indefinitely. They had not been prepared for this response, and when he told them they would just have to wait and hope for the best they were too upset to discuss it with him any further. All they knew about my disease before I entered Homer Folks was either the information Dr. DeMarco had given them, or the horror stories they had heard from other families.

Every Sunday afternoon my parents came during the afternoon visiting hours, which were from two until four. Those two hours went by much too quickly and I was very upset when they had to leave. During the week I gradually adjusted to my new environment, but it was very difficult. I am sure it was the same with all of the other lost children, and the staff had to deal with it all of the time. It was hard for them as well. My grandparents, aunts and uncles would seldom make the long trip to visit me, but still I was luckier than some children who had few or no visitors.

Several years after my mother died, and I was a mother myself, I asked my father how they had coped with my years of hospitalization. We had never talked about it before. "There were so many times when on the way home I had to pull the car off the road." His voice trembled as he relived the past. "Your mother would be crying uncontrollably and I held her in my arms and tried to comfort her."

"After you both left I was also crying," I said. "It was always the same every time you came to see me."

*   *   *

After several weeks my bed was wheeled into one of the children's wards. My temporary isolation had ended. Girls and boys alike watched curiously to see where my bed would be placed. They were anxious to have someone new to talk to and play with. Their beds and nightstands were lined up on both sides. There were toys everywhere. At the end of the ward a very young boy was pounding out a tune on a toy piano and singing along with the music. He was accompanied by another boy beating in rhythm on a small drum.

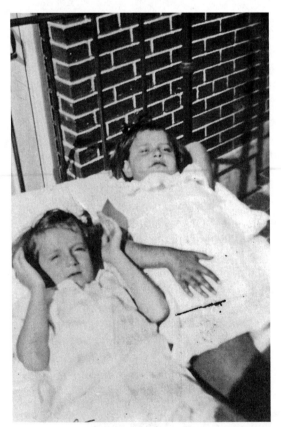

I had not seen or been with any other children in more than a year. Instead of the quiet surroundings that I had become accustomed to, I was now in a very noisy place. Here children laughed and shouted to one another. Hospital employees were constantly coming in and out of the ward.

My bed was placed between two other girls. They wanted to know my name. One of them announced that she was Barbara and the other girl was Sarah. Barbara, the less timid of the two, in a

In 1938, my second year at Homer Folks, I enjoy sunning with my friend Joanne (right).

very loud voice announced to everyone on the ward that the new girl was named Gloria.

"Hi Gloria," they shouted in unison. Some of them giggled as they greeted me. I knew right then that I was going to like it there with all of those kids.

At first I was quite shy and rarely spoke to anyone. However it did not take me long to get used to this noisy active place. Soon I was laughing and shouting, just as boisterous as the rest. My appetite began to improve, and I was happier than I had been in a very long time.

Most of the children were in traction or casts. Children who had tuberculosis of the spine were placed in partial body casts that covered their shoulders down to just above their hips. Some had both spinal and hip tuberculosis and had casts applied that covered most of their bodies. All of them had to lie on an apparatus that resembled an army cot. These special orthopedic frames were placed on top of their mattresses. Frames aided in both positioning and immobilizing a patient. They also allowed the staff to turn a patient easily. Sometimes I heard one of the children crying out in pain at night. It was a common symptom of their illness.

Each of the wards had several doors which led to large open porches that ran the full length of the wards. These doors were wide enough to allow the staff to wheel our beds through. An important part of our treatment was being outdoors in the fresh air and sunlight whenever possible. When the weather was warm our beds were often wheeled out at night, and we slept there until morning. How I loved sleeping there under the stars, breathing in the fresh air, in the hills of Oneonta. In the summer we basked in the sun on the porch, and when the weather was cold nurses provided us with extra blankets. Sometimes we were even allowed to remain outside in a light snow. It was exhilarating to let the snowflakes land on our tongues and to create a white cover over our blankets. No matter what the weather conditions were, I loved being outdoors and never had enough of the porches. There was such a sense of freedom about being outside.

From the porch we had a breathtaking view of the lower campus. We enjoyed watching the activities of the vehicles and people on the grounds beneath the porch. Dopey was with me most of the time. He also liked being outside. My friends were fascinated with him, and Dopey started talking to them as well. I really enjoyed being an amateur ventriloquist.

* * *

At the age of seven my doctors, realizing how important it was to keep my hip immobilized so that it would heal, felt that the best immobilization plan for me was to place me in a spica cast. In this way they hoped that healing would eventually take place and that no further damage would occur. Healing cannot take place if there is movement. Sometimes nature's own method was to splint the muscles in the diseased area in an attempt to bring about immobilization. In this healing process the body attempts to fuse or ankylose the area. Dr. DeMarco had explained this to my parents when I was first placed in traction, but unfortunately nature did not come through for me.

When an orderly came in one morning and lifted me onto a stretcher, I had no idea of where he was taking me. My first thought was that I was probably going to have more x-rays. Instead, he wheeled me into a very strange-looking room. There was nothing in it except a large double sink and a stainless steel table.

When I asked him what the room was for he seemed surprised that no one had told me what was going to take place. He explained that this was a special room where the doctors were going to put a cast on me. None of the doctors or nurses had prepared me for this, and I had no idea of what was going to take place next. A nurse removed all of my clothing and lifted me onto the table. It was very hard, felt so cold, and had a rod in the center fastened to a small metal seat. Once I was positioned on this seat, a small towel was placed between my legs and the rest of the table was lowered. There I was, suspended in midair, while staff members held my ankles, arms, and head. A soft cotton stocking material was placed over the areas of my body that would be covered by the cast.

Spica casts are used to immobilize a limb, especially at the joint. Their size and placement are determined by where the disease has settled. In my case it was put on just below my arms, across and around my chest, and on my left leg leaving only my toes free. On my right leg the cast ended just above my knee. A two-by twelve-inch board was then placed from my left to my right knees, which, because of the spica, were now about two feet apart. This board strengthened the cast and made it easier for the staff when they had to pick me up.

These casts are applied by using gauze bandages in successive v-shaped crossings. Bandages are soaked in warm water mixed with a white powder called plaster of Paris. A paste is formed which hardens into a solid form as it dries. This was a frightening procedure. Although the staff tried to get me to relax it was impossible, and I trembled as the warm bandages were placed around my body.

Following the application of the cast I was lifted back onto the stretcher and returned to the ward. This cast felt heavy and wet, and I could not move. As the cast began to dry it became lighter, but it was still very damp. In order to speed up the drying process, a curved drying apparatus was placed over the cast. It felt like being in a warm tunnel.

That night I again put my covers over my head. It had been a terrifying day. When I fell asleep I had a dream that recurred many times in the years I was at Homer Folks. In this dream I decide to fly out of my window and find my way to my parents' home. I didn't feel like playing with the happy children in my dreams. I wanted my parents. After flying around for a very long time I finally saw the tiny house where they lived. There was a light on in the living room of their upstairs apartment and I was able to look in. My father had fallen asleep in his chair, the newspaper on his lap. My mother was bent over a small table that held a sewing machine. As I watched her hands move quickly over a piece of brightly colored cloth I wondered if she was making another pretty dress for me. When I placed my face as close to the window as possible in order to see

them better, the images of my parents suddenly disappeared. I woke up startled and feverish, once again confined in the warm tunnel.

It took almost a full week for my cast to dry, and when it did it felt very strange. It was so much lighter, and I was able to turn around and lie on my stomach. If I wanted to I could even lie on my right side, but my left leg — which was fully covered with my cast — would then actually be up in the air. Pulling my top bedsheet over me, I shouted to my friends, "Do you think I look like a sailboat?" They said I did and laughed as I rolled back and forth in my imaginary lake between the sheets.

There were many advantages to being in a cast. Now I

Although I am now in my first body cast at Homer Folks in 1937, my mother has no problem lifting me up.

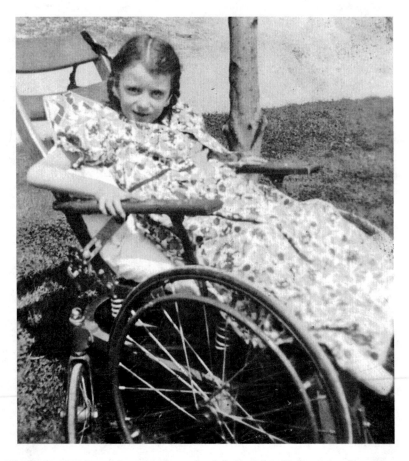

Finally in 1938 I am given my first wheelchair. It is a little uncomfortable as my cast prevents me from sitting up.

was able to move about easily in my bed and was able to be out of bed in a wheelchair for long periods of time. It was also now easier for the staff to pick me up without moving my left leg, now completely immobilized by the cast. My life was now so much different. Now that I had a wheelchair my parents were able to bring me outside of the building and wheel me around the grounds.

Once I was used to the wheelchair and the new cast I got quite daring. Not only my appetite but my energy level improved. When the staff was not around I often got out of the chair and stood up, balancing myself on my right leg. Then I would proclaim to my friends, "Don't I look just like the letter A?"

Every few months the cast had to be removed. How I dreaded this uncomfortable ordeal. First the cast was cut along each side, using a cutting device that resembled large pliers. That was the scariest part as the cutting tool sometimes actually punctured my skin, forcing me to cry out in pain. When this cutting device could not get through tight areas, such as those covering the bones in my ankle and hip, they resorted to using a small and very sharp tool. It looked like a thick pair of scissors. They would hack away for what seemed like hours. Sometimes they cut into my skin, causing it to bleed. I breathed a sigh of relief when they were finally able to lift the entire top of the cast off. For the first time in months the nurses were able to give me a complete bed bath. That was the best part. After bathing and drying me the top of the cast was put back on.

Wide canvas straps were used to connect the bottom and top of the cast. In this way I would still be immobilized, although I was now unable to either lie on my side or turn over by myself. The worst part was not being able to use my wheelchair. It was usually only a few weeks before a new cast was applied. This process went on for many years, until I got so accustomed to having a cast I somehow forgot what it was like to be without one. I felt like a turtle without a shell.

Since our stay at Homer Folks would be a very long one, it was very important for us to continue with our education. Classrooms were located right in the building and children who were not able to walk or use wheelchairs were tutored at their bedside. There were no regular grades, school was an ongoing process and students proceeded at their own pace. Children who were discharged were often able to reenter the grade they would have been in if they had not become ill.

In addition to school there were many recreational activities provided. Sometimes we had picnics on the porch or parties on the ward. Decorations were put up in the day room for every holiday. All types of theme parties were frequently held there as well. It was the custom every Halloween to have a masquerade party in the auditorium. This was followed by a marching parade through the halls for the benefit of those who could not leave their beds. Every child's birthday was celebrated, complete with a cake, ice cream, balloons and games.

We all enjoyed a variety of verbal games that we could play during the long periods when we had to remain in bed. This was especially true at night after the lights were turned off. Many of us were not tired at all, especially since our bedtime was so early. Everyone took turns at playing these games. "I'm thinking of something in this room" was our favorite and was one that even the younger children could take part in.

When we made too much noise a night nurse would come in and try to quiet us down. This rarely worked. After she left someone would whisper, "Gloria, please tell us a story." They loved my ghost stories, and the scarier they were the better. Some brave souls who were able to leave their beds took great delight in sliding across the floor and hiding under the beds of their unsuspecting roommates. In the middle of one of my stories about ghosts, witches, and goblins, they would pop up and scare the unfortunate child whose bed they had hidden under. How I loved this nighttime ritual.

During the day the nurses moved our beds next to one another so we could play together. Before becoming sick we were able to play games like hide and go seek and tag. We rode bicycles and went to playgrounds where there were swing sets and slides. Boys pretended to be cowboys or Indians, while girls pushed doll carriages and pretended they were little mothers. Now our favorite pastime was playing hospital. We were the doctors and nurses, and our patients were our dolls, stuffed animals, or each other. We had medical kits, complete with candy pills, stethoscopes and bandages. Of course I had to take it one step further. One day I placed two wooden trays end to end on my bed. Then I lay on them, pretending they were a frame and that I had tuberculosis of the spine.

Sometimes I used some of my books as hospital beds. Sick paper or small dolls were put in beds which I then lined up just as ours were on our ward. Tissue paper was used for sheets, and cotton handkerchiefs or bits of cloth served as blankets. As I made rounds I checked each patient with the items in my doctor's kit, reviewed their conditions, and prescribed treatment. Sometimes the nurses furnished me with wooden tongue depressors and bits of rolled gauze to play with. Talcum powder mixed with water and soaked in gauze made the plaster I needed to apply casts to my tiny patients. Tongue depressors also made great frames. This was my world, this is what I knew, and like so many of my friends, we never tired of playing hospital. At least we were in control of this one.

On the weekends that my parents did not visit I always received a surprise package during the week. They sent coloring books, paper dolls, and other things they knew I would enjoy. As much as I looked forward to receiving these packages, they did not take the place of a visit. On the weekends that they were unable to come, usually because of bad weather, I missed them so. Most of the visitors knew every child on the ward. When they saw a child who had no visitors they would take the time to talk to them. My parents did the same thing, and always brought special treats for everyone as well. Everyone's favorite was Mom's chocolate cookies. She got so much pleasure passing them out. Of all the food that she brought me, my favorite was her pasta and meatballs. She put them in a vacuum bottle so they would stay warm on the long trip. No hospital meal could ever compare to this delicious Italian food.

On Easter Sunday everyone looked forward to receiving an Easter basket. Some children got one or more, but there were others who did not get any. Relatives on both sides of my family sent baskets and bunnies, and I always had more than anyone else. My parents suggested that I share these and keep my favorite one for myself.

"Here comes Peter Rabbit," my father would shout as he hopped around the ward distributing baskets and other treats to children less fortunate than his daughter. All of the children loved him. He loved to tease them, and they loved the attention.

For Christmas the staff did an amazing job decorating not only our ward, but the halls and day room as well. Each ward had a small tree, and in the day room there was a huge tree that reached to the ceiling. Those of us who were well enough spent weeks making colorful paper chains and ornaments for it. Those who were able helped put them on the tree. Our nurses added multi-colored lights and tinsel. A shining star was placed at the very top by the head doctor. He then turned the day room lights off and the tree lights on. To add to the excitement, presents that arrived by mail or were brought in by visitors ahead of time were placed underneath the tree. They were not to be opened until Christmas morning.

This was my second Christmas away from home. Since my parents had to travel so far to be with me, they decided to come on Christmas Eve and leave the next day. They promised me that they would arrive before my bedtime and that they would be with me when I opened my presents in the morning. I had no idea of where they would sleep, but I did know that sometimes parents were allowed to stay in the building overnight. It did not matter — the only thing that mattered was knowing that I would be with them for a long visit.

My bed was located near the entrance of the ward. On Christmas Eve, every time I heard the elevator door opening, I was sure it was them. By the time bedtime came, they still had not arrived. Although I could hear the voices of staff members talking softly in the hall, I did not hear the voices of my parents. All I heard was the sound of the wind as it whipped around our building during a very heavy snowfall. Eventually I drifted in and out of sleep.

Sometime during the night I heard my parents' voices. They had driven through a terrible snowstorm and had to drive with caution. Occasionally they had been forced to pull the car off the road. Their car was very old and in need of repair, and they were afraid of being stranded on the highway. It was very late and I wanted to call out to them, but realized that by doing so I would wake the other children. Minutes later my parents tiptoed into the ward so they would not disturb those who were sleeping. They explained why they were so late, and then held me close in the dark ward until I fell into a peaceful sleep. It was a Christmas Eve that I often told my own children about — one that I have never forgotten.

In the morning we joined our families in the day room. Now there were even more presents under the tree, so we knew that Santa had not forgotten us. There was a great deal of excitement as the brightly wrapped gifts were opened. It was not the same as being home, but the important thing was that we were with our families. There were volunteers there helping out by taking the place of the families who never visited their children. Special meals on festive trays were brought in for everyone, including our families and volunteers. Despite the fact that our holidays and our lives were so different, it was a very memorable Christmas for me — the difficult part was when my parents had to leave.

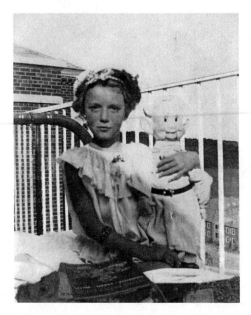

Posing with my favorite doll, Dopey, and wearing the beautiful dress my mother made for my birthday in 1938.

*   *   *

In July of 1939 I left Homer Folks Hospital. Arrangements had been made to transfer me to a sanitarium closer to home. I had been a patient in the children's building for almost two years.

Italian Heritage

During the many years that I struggled to overcome my illness I was fortunate in having a wonderful family support system. In addition to my parents and grandparents, I had many aunts, uncles, and cousins, as well as friends of my parents, who were always there for me. It was because of them that I was able to cope more readily with the unusual circumstances of my childhood. They made me feel loved. They made me laugh. They made me feel better about myself. Of course they spoiled me with so much attention and so many gifts. No doll or toy was too expensive. This was especially true of my grandparents, partly because I was their first grandchild.

Who we are when we are born is not just determined by our genetic makeup, our unique physical features and the inherited diseases that evolve from our genes. It is also influenced by our heritage, our life experiences, and our families. What happened to us in our past shapes our future. My family played a very important role in my becoming the person I am today.

Our family tree has its roots in Italy. Italian immigrants started coming to the village of Seneca Falls in upstate New York in 1884. Most of them, like my grandparents, were from the province of Tuscany or provinces south of its border. At that time the Italian economy was in terrible shape. Jobs were scarce, wages were low, and heavy taxes were imposed on the poor. As word spread that there were good jobs in America, many young men started migrating to this country. At first their goal was to find work, save money, and return to Italy to live a more comfortable life. Most of them changed their minds once they had settled in

Some of my aunts and uncles made the long trip to visit me. Aunt Mary (my godmother), Mom, Aunt Elsie, Uncle Jerry (my godfather) and Uncle Frank.

the village, and they decided to remain in Seneca Falls. Those who had jobs sent money home to help support their families or to bring them to America.

Massimo Giovannini, my maternal grandfather, was one of these young men. He often reminisced about his journey to America. The voyage had taken almost a month and the ship had been extremely uncomfortable. Once they had boarded the ship they were taken below the deck, where they remained for the entire trip. There were no portholes. Everyone had to sleep on the floor, often without blankets or pillows. Food was scarce, and many people became sick and did not survive the trip.

When I asked my grandfather how he got to Seneca Falls, he explained that first he had to go through Ellis Island. From there he had to take a ferry and then a train to get there. Some friends met him at the train station and offered him a place to stay. Those who did not have friends or relatives to stay with had to rent rooms. Then he added with a smile, "I was one of the lucky ones."

Jobs were plentiful in this busy industrialized town, and he had no problem finding work. It was not long before he had saved enough money to purchase a house. Like other immigrants, once he became a home-owner he was able to put down roots and return to the lifestyle and traditions of his homeland. Immigrants usually settled in the same neighborhoods, where they developed a way of life reminiscent of the towns and villages of Italy. These immigrants from Italy, and from other countries as well, took great pride in preserving their heritage. Yet they often found themselves victims of ridicule and discrimination. Not being able to speak English was a major problem. It was years before most of them mastered the language, and some never did. My older relatives spoke very little English, and reverted back to their native language whenever possible.

My grandmother Adele was a very religious and loving person. Her faith in God and her family were her main priorities. She thought those who were not Italian-Americans were unfriendly and often unkind. She called them Americanos and avoided any contact with them.

"We would not even go to Saint Patrick's, the beautiful church in town," she once told me, "so the priest would come to our homes to say Mass and give us communion."

Later, as they started integrating into the community, these dedicated Catholics gradually became members of the parish. My grandfather, a skilled carpenter by trade, installed the huge crucifix in the center of the wall behind the altar of St. Patrick's Church. It is still there today.

In their eagerness to gain acceptance and become "Americanized," many of the immigrants were anxious to become American citizens. They started learning new ways and became successful in many endeavors. Some opened their own business, entered politics, and made numerous contributions to the village. Still, even after becoming "Americanized," they continued to hang on to their traditions and customs.

*   *   *

My maternal grandparents were both from the province of Lucca in northern Italy. They lived in separate villages. My grandmother, Adele Giovanetti, lived in the town of Castle Nuova Garfagnana; my grandfather, Massimo Giovannini, lived in the town of Molazanna. It was not until they immigrated to the states in 1909 and settled in the village of Seneca Falls that they met and were married. Although Adele had seventeen pregnancies, five died at birth or shortly after. Three girls and nine boys survived. Their second child and first daughter, my mother Anne, learned responsibility at a very young age. She helped with the housework, and later on with the care of her younger brothers and sisters.

My grandfather worked at the Seneca Falls Machine Company, but he did not like working in a factory. In order to supplement his income for his increasingly growing family, he used his carpentry skills to do small jobs for people. Eventually he had so many requests for his work he was able to quit working in the factory and he succeeded in developing his own business. Two of his sons, Lee and Mario, joined him later on. They called the family business M. Giovannini and Sons and they remodeled and built some of the finest homes in the village. When my grandfather died my uncles continued on with the business. Among the homes they built was the one my husband and I moved into shortly after we were married. Much of the economic development of Seneca Falls was due to the contributions of people like my grandfather.

My father's parents, Catarina (Pisano) and Donato Didio, also came to the United States from Italy in the early 1900s. They brought with them their only child at the time, my Uncle Roxy. After settling in Auburn they found that even though there were jobs available, the ones that they were offered paid very little.

Donato eventually found employment as a caretaker at the Case Mansion, one of the grand estates that were so prevalent at the time. Catarina, like so many immigrants who did not speak English and had little education, found work at a local knitting mill. They had five more children, three sons and two daughters. My father, Alexander John, was the fifth of six children. None of them were educated beyond the eighth grade. Their parents needed them to either help with the duties at home, or to find jobs to supplement their income.

Their youngest son, Frank, was diagnosed with tuberculosis of his lungs while in his early twenties. His wife, Aunt Elsie, was the aunt who had so generously given my parents the five dollars needed to pay for my first doctor's visit. Now her husband had to leave his young wife and son to recuperate at the Ray Brook Sanitarium near Saranac Lake. Later on he too was transferred to a sanitarium closer to home. After several years he was well enough to return home, but he never fully regained his health. He died in his sleep at the age of forty.

While Uncle Frank was hospitalized, and I was still a patient at Homer Folks, he built a delightful miniature house for me out of matchsticks. He had been a chain smoker, but once he became ill he stopped smoking. I am sure that is why he had so many boxes of unused matchsticks. What better way to use them than to build something for his little niece. Inside this carefully constructed house he built a staircase with a rail to the second floor. A front porch, complete with matchstick posts, surrounded the tiny structure. I spent many happy hours playing with this unique playhouse.

Uncle Frank was not the only member of my family who had tuberculosis of the lungs. My mother's youngest sister, Margaret, was another victim of this contagious disease. Aunt Margaret was admitted to one of the sanitariums I was in.

*   *   *

There are so many more memories of my mother's parents than of my fathers'. This is because I spent much more time with them prior to being hospitalized. Grandpa Massimo was an extremely handsome man. He constantly smoked a pipe. His eyes would twinkle as he sat in his rocking chair and puffed away, filling the room with the poignant aroma of tobacco. Sometimes he lifted me up towards the ceiling and twirled me around until my grandmother made him stop.

"Massimo, Massimo!" she would shout. "Put her down. You're going to hurt her!"

Grudgingly he would put me down — that was until she was out of sight.

When I was at their house it seemed like she was always in the kitchen softly humming the music of her homeland as she cooked and baked for her large family. She loved the opera and listened to her records repeatedly. Like so many immigrants she never quite adjusted to life in this country. She missed being in Italy and fiercely clung to the traditions and language. They were very proud of the region in northern Italy where they had come from, bringing with them the traditions and customs of previous generations.

During World War II many soldiers from Italy were incarcerated in a facility a short distance from Seneca Falls. They were prisoners of war. Most of them were very young. A high wire fence surrounded their living quarters. My grandparents were very upset about this— and about the war. Two of their own sons were serving in the army in Europe at the time. Along with other Italian families, they made frequent trips to bring these soldiers food that included their favorite Italian dishes. They talked to them in their native tongue, and reminisced about Italy. No one ever dared mention the name Mussolini to my grandmother for fear that she would faint.

*   *   *

My mother got married without her parents' approval. They felt that she was too young. She was only eighteen, and my father was just two years older. He did not have a job or any prospects of employment. In order to help his own family out he had dropped out of school in the fifth grade to work as a delivery boy. Since his family all lived twenty miles away and he did not own a car, they were afraid that they would see little of their daughter. Shortly after they eloped my father's parents found them an apartment near them. They had to rely on others to drive them to Seneca Falls to visit.

When I was born in 1931 my parents had very little money. Since the collapse of the stock market in 1929 they were unemployed, along with millions of Americans. My mother found work in a local shoe factory. When she lost her job she found another one in a factory that made dresses. There she soon became a skilled seamstress. This was a turning point in her career. With her newly acquired skill she began earning extra money by taking in sewing. Women came to our apartment to either have alterations done on their clothes, or have new ones made. They brought their own patterns and material. It was not long before she had so many customers she had to sew until late at night to keep up with the demand. It was exhausting work, but she was ambitious and determined to improve our lives. It seemed as though nothing would stand in her way.

Gloria Mary Didio, born in Auburn, New York, in October 1931. I was my parents' first child and the only grandchild at the time.

With my mother working so many hours, she had little time to take care of me. This meant that my father had to take over. Today this is called being "Mr. Mom." While my mother had a lot of experience in taking care of her younger brothers and sisters, such was not the case for my father. He did the best he could, but he desperately wanted to find a job so that my mother would not have to work so hard and could be home more to take care of me.

One day, shortly after my admission to Mercy, my father came home very excited. He told my mother she would never believe what had happened to him. He had finally found work, thanks to President Roosevelt. My mother was obviously thrilled with this news, but could not understand what President

Roosevelt had to do with it. My father explained with pride that the president had a program called the New Deal. They had listened to the president on the radio explaining the new economic and social programs he was creating. One of them was the WPA (Works Progress Administration). It was because of this program that my father now had a job. He worked on the construction and repair of buildings in the area. Yet even with both of them now employed, they could barely meet their expenses. Somehow they did manage to save enough money to pay for my follow-up visits to the doctor and for my medications. Members of both families were very supportive in helping them out financially, even though they were also struggling.

When my family found out that I was being transferred much closer to home they were so happy. Most of them had not seen me since my discharge from Mercy. Once again they resumed their visits, and the support system was once more in place.

Biggs Memorial Hospital

When I was told I was leaving Homer Folks I asked my parents why I couldn't just go home. Since I did not feel sick, I could not understand why I had to be transferred to a different hospital. I liked it right where I was. They explained that the new hospital was much closer to home. They promised me that because of this they would be able to visit me more often. My grandparents, aunts and uncles would also visit me more.

Nothing they said to me mattered. I did not want to leave my young friends and the staff at Homer Folks that I had become so accustomed to. They had all been like a family to me. Now I was going to be separated forever from my second hospital family. Memories of the fine nuns at Mercy had already begun to fade, and now I had lost two beloved substitute families.

It was 1939 when I was admitted to Biggs Memorial Hospital. Biggs was located in upstate New York, a short distance from the small picturesque city of Ithaca, just forty minutes from my home. It was built to meet the needs of many counties in the Finger Lakes region. This 250-bed hospital took four years to build, and the first patient was admitted in 1936. In addition to the main building where I was first admitted, the campus included a children's building that was called simply "H." There was a nurses' dormitory, several houses for staff members, a power plant and a greenhouse. Although the buildings were spread out over nearly two-hundred acres on gently sloping hills, just like the ones at Homer Folks, they were much more attractive. Perhaps it was the fact that the stately vine-covered Tudor-style buildings resembled a resort in the countryside of England rather than a sanitarium.

Biggs was dedicated to Dr. Herman M. Biggs, a physician, statesman of public health, and pioneer in the field of preventative medicine. Dr. Biggs had been the state commissioner of health in New York State. He did more for the prevention and administrative control of tuberculosis than any other person in this country at the time.

This was to be my next home. By now, after being in two hospitals, I had become fairly well adjusted to living away from home. It had become a way of life for me, a life of constant unending confinement. Memories of my short stay in kindergarten, of what it was like to walk and run, to ride a tricycle or visit a playground, gradually began to fade. Now I no longer expected a parent to tuck me in at bedtime, to read bedtime stories, to hold me, or to give me a good night kiss. It simply did not happen. In their place, I clung to my dolls, and my dreams.

Instead of riding with my parents this time, I was put on a stretcher and wheeled into a hospital transportation vehicle. It may have been an ambulance. Although I have no recollection of that ride, I can just imagine how frightened I must have been. When we arrived, the driver backed the vehicle up to a loading dock at the back of the hospital. My parents were there, anxiously waiting for me. My father greeted me with a forced smile. He held my hand as he looked down at my tiny figure, my body almost totally covered with the spica cast, and my other hand clinging to the side of the stretcher. Tears were running down my cheeks as he kissed me and whispered in my ear, assuring me that I would like it here much better than Homer Folks. Then my mother leaned over, placed a kiss on each of my cheeks, and told me how much she loved me. With both parents at my side, I began to feel a little better. An orderly met us inside and took us on an elevator up to the ward where I would be staying. Once again, I was put in a private room where I would remain in isolation for several weeks. This time we did not ask about the children's building. We had been assured that I would be transferred there. First more laboratory tests and x-rays would have to be taken and my case thoroughly reviewed.

My new room was much nicer than the room I had at Homer Folks. It had a double window where I could look out and see a lake. It looked so close, but was actually several miles away at the end of tree-covered grasslands with winding streams that flowed into it. Tiny moving objects that I could see on the lake turned out to be boats, and sailboats were especially visible. When I looked out at the other side of the lake I thought that was where the world ended. This time when my parents had to leave they reminded me that now that I was so much closer to home they would be back in a few days.

There was a constant parade of nurses, doctors, orderlies and visitors outside of my door. Often they stopped in to talk to me. It was not as lonesome here as it had been in my private room at Homer Folks. In addition to new admissions, all of the patients on this ward were very ill. I could hear their constant coughing, especially at night.

Did they have colds?

Why were they coughing so much at night?

When I asked one of the nurses about this she told me that they had a different kind of sickness than I had. She said that, although they sounded like they had colds, it was their sickness that made them cough so much. Even though I found this hard to comprehend, it made me feel uncomfortable.

What would happen if I got their sickness?

Would I start to cough as well?

My isolation continued for several weeks while more laboratory tests and x-rays were taken. After my case was reviewed, my parents were asked to meet with my new doctor. This time they were not expecting bad news as my general health seemed to be so much better. Their worries, however, were far from over. He told them that my latest stereoscopic pelvic x-rays showed bizarre changes involving the left side of the pelvis, including the head and neck of the femur and a portion of the shaft. There had been massive destruction of bone which had caused the entire head and neck of the femur to be absorbed. One area had a cystic appearance. These changes were not consistent with a tubercular process. Complete sets of x-rays were sent to Albany to rule out a neoplastic growth — a giant cell tumor. Cancer had to be ruled out.

This time there was no consoling my parents. How could I have tuberculosis and cancer? It seemed like an eternity to them until the report came back negative for any malignancy. Earlier diagnosed tuberculosis had been correct. That was very good news. However, these x-rays also revealed that all of the attempts to immobilize my hip had failed and the disease was still widespread. It would be a very long time before I would leave the sanitarium, and I had already been hospitalized for more than three years.

During my isolation, I again found that I had no interest in eating. Here the nurses also did everything they could to encourage me to finish the food on my tray. Nothing seemed to work. Now that I was older I was much more daring, and I would often cleverly wrap my food up in my paper napkin and toss it into the wastebasket. For breakfast the food I disliked the most was hot cereal. When I discovered that the thick rubber cover on my nightstand was detachable, I began hiding the cereal underneath it. It was not discovered while I was there.

At Homer Folks I had attended school where I read children's books at a level several grades higher than the one I would have been in if I had not been hospitalized. My parents were constantly buying me new books, but they were never enough. Sometimes I read and re-read them so often I had much of the text memorized. Soon after my arrival, one of the hospital's librarians rolled a cart filled with children's books into my room. She placed it right next to my bed so that I could reach them. When I looked at the large selection of books, I was ecstatic. Since she only delivered books once a week, she told me that I could take as many of them as I liked. There were so many choices— wonderful books with stories and illustrations to delight the heart of any child. These were now all available to me. While I escaped from the real world at night to fly over rooftops, reading was my escape during the day.

When the librarian found out I was especially interested in the lake I could see from my window she told me that it was called Cayuga Lake. She explained that this lake was the longest of a group of lakes called the Finger Lakes. Years ago ancient Indian tribesmen believed that these lakes were shaped by the imprint of God's fingers and were blessed. That is why they were called the Finger Lakes. Scientists, she explained, believed that these lakes were formed from huge blocks of ice called glaciers a long time ago. As they melted these lakes were formed. Her explanation was interesting, yet I still liked to believe that the Indians' version was the true one.

When she returned the following week she brought me a book about the Ice Age and glaciers. Still I could not get the fascinating Indian version out of my mind.

One sunny morning a young man dressed in a white uniform wheeled a stretcher into my room. He had blond curly hair and greeted me with a huge grin on his face. His name was Peter and he told me that we were going to go outdoors. Peter was one of the orderlies that worked on the floor I was on. It was his assignment to take me outside. It had been such a long time since I had been able to leave my room. When I asked him if he was taking me to a different room he shook his head and told me no. Instead, he said, we were going on a great adventure to a place much more interesting.

Peter wheeled me into an elevator and we headed toward the top floor. Our destination turned out to be a flat stone-covered roof on top of the seven-foot tower located near the entrance of the hospital.

He explained that there were many rooms in the tower. Some of the people who worked there stayed in them. His room was on the top floor.

How wonderful it was to be outside in the fresh air! We could look down and see the entire campus. Peter pointed to a building not far from the building, we were in. As he wheeled me as close to the roof as he dared, he told me that it was the children's building, where I would be going. Then he suggested that we shout as loud as we could, over the rooftops of the buildings below. Peter loved to sing and he encouraged me to join him. Our favorites were *Row, Row, Row Your Boat* and *Old MacDonald Had a Farm*. Sometimes we pretended we were on a great mountain and had to be on the lookout for enemy soldiers. He made me laugh as he pranced around the roof shouting, "I am Peter the Great, and this young lady is my princess." I was a princess again! No one had called me princess in a very long time.

Peter gathered some of the brightly colored pebbles that covered the floor of the roof. He then put them in a cup for me to take back to my room. Pebbles that were not as colorful were tossed into the air and onto the ground below.

When we finally had to return to my room, and as we got off the elevator, Peter would look around to see if anyone was nearby. Then to my absolute delight — when there were no staff members in sight — he would run swiftly with my stretcher. Peter the Great was my friend, my only friend at that time. We made several trips to the rooftop while I was waiting to be admitted to the children's building, and my memories of these trips have remained with me.

One Sunday my grandparents from Seneca Falls brought my young uncles to visit me. You can imagine how excited I was. I had not had any contact with children during these many weeks of isolation. Some of my uncles were not much older than I was. None of them were allowed to either enter the building or come to my room on the second floor. My grandfather moved my bed over to the window and opened it so that I could see my uncles. They had come right from church and were still dressed in their white shirts and dark pants. This did not stop them from running, jumping, doing cartwheels and playing tag. How I longed to be down there on the lawn with them, to go home with them, to be a part of their life. They loved showing off, and when I shouted down to them to see who could run the fastest they kept racing until every one of them had won at least once.

When it was time for them to leave I felt a knot in my stomach and

The front of the children's building (H) at Biggs Memorial Hospital in Ithaca, New York, in 1939. I am glad to be so much closer to home.

a feeling of hopelessness, of sadness. Perhaps it would have been better if they had not come at all.

*   *   *

After several weeks, when all of my x-ray and laboratory tests were completed and reviewed, I was told that I was now going to be transferred to the children's (H) building. It was common practice for the state to use letters to identify buildings. That explained why the long extensions in the main building were lettered as well.

On the morning of the transfer, a nurse placed all of my belongings on my bed. As she placed my beloved Dopey at my side, she told me that they were going to miss me and my little friend as well. Peter came in to wheel my bed to the loading ramp in back of the hospital. He took my hand and said he was taking his beautiful princess on yet another great adventure. It sounded exciting, but my eyes filled with tears as I asked if I would ever see him again. He told me that he did not work in the children's building, but noticing my tears promised that he would come to visit me when he had a day off. That seemed to satisfy me as he leaned over and placed a kiss on my forehead. Then he placed a small cup of brightly colored pebbles into my hand. My memories of Peter, like the ones of Sister Mary Margaret, gradually faded away. I never saw him again either.

A large covered truck backed up into the ramp and the driver got out and helped Peter roll me in. It was very dark in the truck, and as it headed for the children's building, I clung to the sides of my bed — anxious and afraid. It was a short ride, and as I lay there I thought about leaving behind the friendly librarian and Peter — whom I would miss — and the dried-up cereal under my nightstand — which I would not.

During my stay at H I made many trips back and forth to the main building for tests, but none would be as scary as this first one. Once we reached our destination, the driver backed up to a loading dock. We were met by a nurse who wheeled me to the room where I would be staying.

Patients with skeletal tuberculosis, children and adults, were housed at H. There were very few patients admitted here with this type of the disease. That was because tuberculosis of the bones and joints, and other areas outside of the lungs, make up just 25 percent of cases. Most of the patients there were ambulatory women with pulmonary tuberculosis, the form that is responsible for over 75 percent of cases. These women were in the final stage of their cure. Their tuberculosis was caused by a different mycobacterium than mine that was called *Mycobacterium tuberculosis*. If these women did not suffer a relapse, and all of their tests became negative, they would be discharged and able to return home. Later on I would learn much more about their illness. There were a few patients there that had both types of tuberculosis.

Large wards with long open porches, similar to the ones at Homer Folks, were located on both floors of this building. Not far from these wards there were single and double rooms on each side of the corridors. When the nurse wheeled my bed into one of these single rooms, I was once again disappointed to find I would not be with other children. This time I said nothing. When I looked across the hall I saw a boy about my age sitting up in his bed. When he spotted me he greeted me and told me his name was Francis. He asked what my name was and I shouted back "Gloria." Now that I had another child to talk to I was the happiest I had been since leaving Homer Folks.

Francis and I became best friends, yelling back and forth whenever our doors were open. He came to visit me in his wheelchair every day. We played board games and cards and spent hours drawing and coloring. He never told me what kind of tuberculosis he had; perhaps he did not know.

In the innocence of childhood, we had a natural curiosity regarding the physical differences between girls and boys. We decided to satisfy our curiosity by exposing ourselves. Neither one of us were impressed with the other's parts. Francis promised me he would not tell anyone, but the temptation was too great. Eventually word of our exploration got back to the staff. We were not allowed to be together for a week. Apparently the staff felt we had already seen enough of one another.

Once I was given a wheelchair I spent time in Francis's room watching him make model airplanes. He used balsam wood, thin translucent paper and glue. Assembling these tiny aircraft was a very intricate and detailed process. When I asked if I could help he always said no, reminding me that after all I was just a girl. Eventually he gave in and we spent hours in the construction of his miniature squadron.

* * *

One thing I was gradually learning is that when you are in a sanitarium for a long time you do not always stay in the same room, ward, or even building. There were some instances where patients were even moved to a different sanitarium. No one was given a choice. Over the years I experienced many of these moves. Most of the time the placement had to do with the stage of treatment you were in. There were a few instances that I can recall where members of the staff granted permission for a patient to move to a room or ward of their choice. However, by now I was resigned to the fact that I would be moved to a different room or ward at the discretion of the staff. It was not long before I was moved to a double room in front of the building. When I looked out of my window I could see the room where Francis was. Now I was further away from him, but I did see him nearly every day either in class or in the day room.

Much to my delight I now had a roommate. Her name was Jean. Of course I would have preferred rooming with Francis, but boys and girls were not allowed to share rooms. Jean had tuberculosis of the spine, the most common form of bone tuberculosis. Her cast covered her upper body from just below her neck to her hips, and she had to lie on a frame day and night. In this way, she could be turned over by the staff. I felt so sorry for her, and had no interest in pretending that I was on a frame. She did not have the freedom of movement that I did, and had to be transported on a stretcher.

It did not take me long to discover that I did not have as much in common with her. How I had enjoyed being with Francis, helping him build model airplanes and playing with toy soldiers, tanks and guns. It seems that despite my very large collection of dolls I was actually more interested in toys that boys generally played with. Perhaps I was a tomboy. Francis and I had been very competitive in the games we played. We enjoyed teasing and playing jokes on each other. Now I had a rather quiet roommate whose favorite pastime was playing with her large collection of dolls. Although I had accumulated an even larger collection than she had, I seldom played with them anymore. Jean was happy to take them off my hands. There were only two dolls that I played with. One was a replica of General Douglas MacArthur —fully clothed in uniform. His right arm was permanently bent in a salute. Then there was the delightful Dopey, who recently had his picture taken with me on my birthday. My parents had contacted a professional photographer to take this picture. In it I am on the porch sitting on my bed and wearing a new pink dress that my mother had made for me. Dopey was cradled in my arms. Today Dopey is on display in our house, along with this picture.

There was not much to see from my window, but it was my view of the outside world. One day I looked down and saw two young boys riding their bicycles on the circular drive near the entrance. In order to get their attention I called down to them. They did not answer, so I shouted as loud as I could and asked them to look up to my window. When they saw me they said that their names were Warren and Deagan. They both lived in houses on the grounds of the hospital. Their fathers were doctors and worked at Biggs, where special houses and other residences were provided for them.

These two boys started riding their bikes over to visit me nearly every day during the summer. Often they raced each other around the circular drive. Sometimes they played catch and even threw the ball up to my open window, encouraging me to try and catch it. When I finally did they clapped their hands and even did a cartwheel or two.

One windy day they brought kites and ran back and forth to show me how they made them fly. After that I asked my parents for a kite. They seemed surprised, but on their next visit they brought me a large red kite. On windy days I tossed the kite out of my window and hung tightly to the attached string. My kite never did take off, and even though I was disappointed I had fun just trying. When school started the boys didn't come around as often and I missed them so much.

Two young adults, Elena and Jerry, each had a room right across the hall from us. They both had spinal tuberculosis but did not have to lie on frames as Jean did, although they each had a cast like hers on their upper bodies. Elena also had tuberculosis in both lungs. A petite, outgoing young woman, she was always laughing and was very popular with both the other patients and staff. She had many visits from them, but she rarely had company from outside of the hospital. She never mentioned her family. Perhaps she was an orphan. No one ever talked about it. My parents loved her and took the time to visit her every time they came.

Jerry was even quieter than Jean. He was a very pleasant man and was always either reading books or writing poetry. If I turned over on my stomach and turned myself around I could look into their rooms and talk to them. Jerry encouraged me to read some of the books I was reading aloud to them. They were a captive audience. In return Jerry would read us some of his poetry. My favorite one, which appeared in the hospital newspaper, was about giving thanks for his faith, the wonders of nature, and for life itself. This beautiful poem was written by a young man who was very ill, who had been hospitalized for years, and who had given up his dream to be a teacher and perhaps even a published poet. He spent his days encased in a body cast, and sleepless nights in so much pain. I often heard his bell at night, followed by the footsteps of a night nurse who entered his room to bring him his medications. Yet Jerry gave thanks, and I have never forgotten him and his inspiring poem.

Elena told jokes and often made up humorous stories about the staff, most of which were greatly exaggerated. She told amusing tales of the nurses who she claimed were actually witches without brooms, and doctors who were warlocks. We had our own little literary group and so much fun as well.

*   *   *

Classes in grades one through twelve were held in the schoolroom on the first floor. It was a regular classroom with desks and two large blackboards. Children who were ambulatory or in wheelchairs used the desks, while others were wheeled in on stretchers. Some of the chairs had been removed so that those in wheelchairs could pull right up to their desk. There was only one teacher but, since there were not that many children, she was able to teach everyone. Older children took turns helping the younger ones. It reminded me of the one-room schools that I often read about. Our school day was limited to just a few hours because rest was such an important part of our recovery. When I tried to bring Dopey with me into the classroom our teacher said I had to leave him in my room. It would be too distracting for the other children. He would just have to learn his lessons from me.

Most of us welcomed going to school because it relieved the monotony of institutional living. Despite all of the activities that were provided we still had way too much time on our hands. What we lost in our education in not having a longer class day I believe we gained because we spent so much time reading. At least I know that this was true in my case.

A large day room was located in the center of the second floor right across from the nurses' station. All of the children either walked or were wheeled into this room nearly every day. It was just like the one at Homer Folks, and the same celebrations were held for every holiday and birthday. In the winter we had indoor picnics. There were many toys and books for us to enjoy. Someone had donated a huge dollhouse that opened from the top and was fully furnished. It was one of the favorite toys, especially since it was easy to reach down into from a wheelchair.

There were not as many staff members in this building and there was only one nurses' station. It was located on the second floor right across from the day room. Our nurses had a private room downstairs next to the schoolroom. After all of the patients were settled in for the

Our annual Halloween party in the day room at Biggs in 1941. I am the tallest one in back.

night they went to their room until morning. If anyone needed them there were call bells on each bed that rang in their room.

Francis and I were always trying out new and innovative ways of doing things. We came up with the idea of using two tin cans as telephones by connecting them with string. We could not figure out how to get this string across the building to connect from his room to mine. A friendly maintenance man helped us out by having me hold on to my can and drop the other to the ground, where he then threw it up for Francis to grab from his second-story window. It took several attempts before we were connected. These makeshift phones did not work very well, so we decided to try something else. We made up a code system and, with the use of flashlights, communicated with each other after dark.

Our most daring escapade was one that was weeks in planning. We decided to leave our rooms late at night and to meet in the day room. We hid food, including snacks and peanut butter sandwiches, in the large closet in this room where our rendezvous was to take place. On the night we planned to meet we waited until we heard the elevator. This was our signal that the nurse was going down to her room on the first floor for the night. Keeping awake so late was the hardest part of this exciting adventure. We used our flashlights to signal when we would leave our rooms and then took them with us. Our plan was to throw a blanket on the floor next to our beds. Then we would lower ourselves onto them, lie down on our stomachs, and use our arms to push us on our magic carpets over the tiled floors.

This was the most mischievous and exciting thing I had ever done, and everything went according to plan. Since the floors were frequently waxed and buffed we were able to glide swiftly towards the day room. It was so quiet and the only thing we could hear was the ticking of the large clock which hung over the entrance of the day room. We giggled and whispered as we slid into the day room and hid in the closet. While we devoured our refreshments we plotted our next adventure. We agreed that it should take place during the day. No one ever found out about this one. We wondered if our luck would one day run out. Another transfer several months later put an end to our plans.

Soon I was able to use a wheelchair for part of the day and allowed to wheel myself all over the building. Wheelchairs then were quite different from the ones used today. They were made out of wood and wicker and were heavier and harder to manage. Still, they were sturdily built, and in a very short time I found that I could manage mine quite easily. Because of the spica cast I was unable to sit up in it. The back was lowered in a raised but slanted position and one leg of the chair was raised.

Sometimes I got on the elevator and went to the first floor. There did not seem to be the strict supervision here that there had been at Homer Folks. Patients at H did not need very much nursing care; most of them were ambulatory, so there was no need for a large staff.

Once I was comfortable going downstairs on the elevator I discovered an elegant day room just across from the main entrance. This absolutely beautiful room fascinated me. There were oriental rugs, exquisite furniture and lamps, along with interesting oil paintings on the walls. Three ships, replicas of the ones Christopher Columbus had sailed on, were displayed on one of the long mahogany tables. At the end of the room there was a brick fireplace where the staff often roasted marshmallows and popped corn for the children. French doors led to open porches that extended across the entire back of the building on both floors. They were connected by an outside staircase. Across from this room were two much smaller rooms which were used as game rooms. One contained an upright piano. It seemed that the state had done everything to make our stay here as pleasant as possible.

One of the areas of H that was off limits was the basement. It was forbidden territory, and we had been warned not to go down there. Francis and I had talked about this the night we had met in the day room closet. Since we had access to the elevator and were not that closely supervised, it was only a matter of time before curiosity got the best of us. It was just too much of a temptation. What could possibly be down there that we were not supposed to see?

Francis and I led a small group of children to the elevator and headed for the basement. So far none of our escapades had been discovered, so we were fairly confident that we would not get caught. We decided to go during a period of time when the staff would be too busy to notice our absence. When we got off the elevator and entered the basement it was very dark. There were no lights on. As we proceeded into this unfamiliar territory there was a strong unfamiliar smell. Then we heard some strange noises.

Petie, the youngest member of the expedition, was frightened and wanted to go back upstairs before we got caught. Francis was cross with him but told him he could go, with a warning not to tell anyone or he would have him to deal with. Since Petie as a rule was afraid of everything and everybody we were confident that he would not tell anyone where we were.

Once Petie got on the elevator we made our way towards where the sounds and unusual odor were coming from. We entered a room where there were small animals (guinea pigs) in cages. When we approached their cages we noticed they all had gaping holes in their sides. We did not realize that these animals were used in laboratory studies of tuberculosis. Frances suggested that we rescue one of them and hide it in the day room closet. We were desperate to have any kind of a pet. However, since the cages were locked, we were unable to remove any of them. This was not only lucky for us, but also for the pathetic looking furry creatures looking out at us with such sad eyes. This was no doubt the most dangerous adventure we had, although we did not realize it. All of these experimental animals had been injected with active tuberculosis and were used for the diagnosis of tuberculosis. Since we could not get them out of their cages we never went there again.

We made frequent trips to the basement once we realized that no one really knew we were down there. It was uncharted territory, dark and spooky, the perfect place for us to explore. One winter we noticed a number of very large and small boxes in the hallway leading to where our little friends were caged. When we examined the boxes, even opening a few of the smaller ones, we realized that they contained a playground set, complete with swings and slides. We never told anyone about this, and when spring came and the set was put up outside we pretended to be surprised.

I realized that it would be impossible for me to use the slide, but I was determined to use the swing. Balancing myself as well as I could in my cast, I sat on the narrow seat, but as I kept slipping off I realized that it just was not going to work for me. Still it was fun watching some of the others who were able to use this playground equipment. It was then that I began to realize even more how limited I was in my ability to take part in many of the activities that children enjoy so much. For the rest of my life I have spent time watching others, children and adults, do things that I wanted to be able to do. Sometimes I would be asked to push the children on their swings. This was easy to do from my wheelchair, and I delighted in making them go higher and higher until they cried out for me to stop.

Patients published a monthly newspaper, the *Tower News*, which was originally called the *Biggs Eye-View*. Doctors and other staff members submitted articles that they felt would be helpful to patients in learning about their disease and how to cope with the long difficult cure. There was really nothing in this paper that was of interest to me or the other children. Most of the information contained news of people and events in the main building, and the medical articles were too difficult for us to understand.

One day I was approached by one of the editors and asked if I would like to write a monthly column about the children in H. That was when, at the age of nine, my love of writing actually began. I called my column "*Small Fry*," a nickname Peter had given me.

Here is an excerpt: "Tomboy Gloria Didio feels at home in the overalls she wore in the Revolt at Safe Gable that the children presented for the patients at H. With over twenty dresses Gloria Didio still wishes for another pair of overalls. What will Gloria Didio do if they ration tires for wheelchairs and also if they make a speed limit for them?" My favorite was "Buy your Stamps and Lick the Japs!" When I was about nine years old my first poem appeared in the paper. Of course I was influenced by Jerry, our resident poet.

"A Spook Party"

On Monday night about six
you would have found "Small Fry" in an awful fix.
The nurses going here and there,
taking costumes everywhere
so each would have something to wear.
The jack-o'-lantern gave us our light
upon this very spooky night.
On the blackboard was a bat.
On the fence post sat a cat.
Did you ever see anything look scarier than that?
In came Petie in a stocking cap,
ready, I'm sure, for his all night nap.
Next came Kenneth, a soldier brave
doing his best to look quite grave.
Frances Brown with long curly hair
and baby Frances Tratt made quite a cute pair.
Gloria Didio as a dead end kid,
her black eye was larger than her own eyelid.
A ghost and a pirate made up the rest.
Who these were it was hard to guess.
After our fill of cider, doughnuts, and candy,
we were off to bed thinking the party was just dandy.

Jerry loved my first attempt at poetry, but then he seemed to like everything I wrote.

* * *

My treatment during my stay here was exactly the same as it had been at Homer Folks. At Biggs the orthopedic doctors from a group in Syracuse came in once a month to examine us. Dr. Robert Severson was one of these doctors who managed my care. He was a very kind man and seemed truly interested in me, unlike so many other doctors I had encountered during the past several years. At first he made no changes in my treatment. He continued to order the application of spica casts. They had to be changed more frequently than most because I was unusually active — as most tomboys tend to be.

In 1941 Dr. Severson scheduled a meeting with my parents. Although the latest x-rays had shown slight improvement in bone formation, my hip had retained only one-third of its original range of motion. This was the best news they had received in a long time, but the healing that needed to take place depended on continued immobilization of the diseased area and preventing movement of the joint. This would prevent further destruction of the part and diminished the likelihood of spreading the disease to other parts of the body. It would give my body a chance to heal the lesions that kept multiplying and never seemed to disappear. My parents wondered what would happen next and asked him if my treatment would be the same. Dr. Severson explained that my treatment would continue as it had been, but that in a month he was going to have my cast removed for a while. They were going to apply five to seven pounds of traction. After two months he would have more x-rays taken and, if things had not changed, he would make a decision on what to do next.

Those next few months were difficult for me. Lying in bed all the time and being unable to use my wheelchair was like starting all over again. It did not matter to me at all that my condition had somewhat improved. Time went by slowly and I became more and more depressed each day. Now I had to attend school on a stretcher and could no longer write on the blackboard or help the teacher hand out assignments.

Why is this happening to me?

I just do not understand it.

Soon I began to lose interest in school, my friends, and even in reading. Once again I began losing weight. Even Dopey could not cheer me up. When my parents visited I put on what I call my happy face. This was something that I continued to do even as an adult so that people would not know how I was really feeling, especially those who were close to me.

When the two months were up there were no changes. My condition seemed to have stabilized. This time when the traction was removed

I really did not mind at all when I was told I had been scheduled to have another cast put on. For the first time I actually looked forward to this uncomfortable procedure, and the independence I would get once it dried.

At H there was not as much emphasis on having us outside on the porches. We still spent a lot of time there but never overnight, and never when the weather was cold. While we still spent hours in the sun, I began to notice that the ambulatory women always sat in the shade.

What I did not know at the time was that patients with tuberculosis of the lung were not permitted to have their chests exposed to the sun. It did not matter that their chests were covered. Apparently it had something to do with the chance of the disease spreading further into the lungs. This was the exact opposite of the theory that my type of tuberculosis was improved by sun exposure. Ambulatory patients were free to go outside of the building whenever they chose. They had their meals in the dining room. Often I thought how nice it would be to eat in this room with other people, but it never happened. None of the children were allowed to have their meals there. We always had to eat in our rooms.

There was a small wooden radio on my nightstand. I had music on most of the time and was familiar with all of the popular music of the day. On Sunday December 7, 1941, I had my radio on and the music was interrupted. President Roosevelt was telling the nation about the shocking news of the attack on Pearl Harbor. Following that I heard radio announcers talking about a country called Japan and the terrible thing they had done to the United Sates. There was talk about a big war — it was called World War II. When I asked my parents to explain it to me they made very light of it. My father assured me that it was nothing to worry about, that it would soon be over, and that the United States would easily win. Everything would go back the way it was before the attack. What he told me was not what I was hearing on the radio. People were calling the soldiers from Japan the Japs and were saying scary things about them.

My uncle Aldo, one of my mother's brothers, was an Army sergeant stationed in Europe. He wrote to me often and sent me a large framed picture of himself in his uniform. His picture was on my nightstand right next to my radio. One of his brothers, Joseph, was also in the army and stationed in Europe. I was so proud of these two uncles.

Now instead of collecting paper dolls I started to collect miniature toy soldiers, jeeps, tanks and airplanes. A battleground was spread out over my bed. Army medical teams and ambulances were stationed nearby in case anyone was wounded. Hills were formed with the use of pillows placed under my bedspread. Talcum powder made wonderful snow. It made quite a mess, but the staff did not seem to mind. Sometimes they even joined me in playing with my sweet-smelling snowbound troops.

I was terrified that the Japanese soldiers would attack the hospital. In order to feel safe at night I asked my parents for an army rifle. My grandfather made a replica of one using wood. Every night I placed it at my side in case the Japs entered my room. Each floor had large bathrooms with shower stalls and lockers. It was easy for me to push my wheelchair up to the sinks to wash up. Usually there were other patients in this room, but sometimes I was the only one in there. Up until the war this had never bothered me. Now I was terrified to be in there alone because I was afraid that enemy soldiers were hiding in the lockers or shower stalls.

Although my fascination with the war was sometimes frightening, I also found it equally exciting. Now I pretended that my wheelchair was either a jeep or other army vehicle. Sometimes it was an army ambulance racing through enemy fire to rescue wounded soldiers, or a tank racing up and down the hospital corridors looking for the Japs! Certainly I was a brave soldier, except when I was alone in the shower room.

One day I decided to convert my wheelchair into an airplane. Perhaps if I could put wings on it I could make it fly. Not far from H one of the staff houses was on a hill. There was a long sloping driveway extending from the garage to the main road. This would make an excellent runway. In order to build this wheelchair-plane I would need some heavy pieces of cardboard and twine from the stockroom. An orderly, who had no idea what I needed these for, brought me as much cardboard and twine as I needed. He asked me if I was building a doll house. I told him it was to be a surprise so he did not ask me again. The pieces of the cardboard to be used as wings were very hard to cut, but I talked an occupational therapist into letting me borrow some special scissors. Once the wings were complete I was able to attach them to my arm rests with the twine.

Every plane needs a propeller, so I fashioned one out of the same cardboard and attached it to the foot of my left leg rest. Since this leg rest was always elevated to accommodate my cast, I was sure that it would spin faster there. When I was finished, I removed the parts and hid them in my locker — hoping the Japs would not find them.

On the morning of takeoff, I balanced these pieces on my lap and

Santa Claus Doesn't Forget Children Ill in Hospital

Santa is handing me a gift at the children's Christmas party at Biggs in 1939.

pushed myself outside. No one noticed me leaving the building. They were used to my constant going in and out. My rifle was at my side just in case I ran into enemy territory.

There was no car in the driveway when I arrived at the "airport," so I was sure no one was home. It was hard work to push myself to the top while trying to keep the airplane parts from falling out of my lap. After reaching the top I turned the chair around, put on my brakes, and attached all of the parts. My carefully thought out plan was to release the brakes, zoom down the driveway, and gather enough speed to soar into the sky. Well, I was right about one thing. When I released the brakes the chair did indeed zoom down, gathering speed as it raced towards the road. However I never did soar into the sky. Instead, once I reached the road, I quickly turned it towards the right and, wheeling my chair as fast as I could, made my way towards the entrance to the hospital. Miraculously there were no cars approaching, and I did not tip over or crash into the main road. My first attempt as a pilot was the talk of H for months to come. Needless to say I never tried this again — especially when threatened by the hospital's director himself that my airplane would be impounded if I did. This man was even scarier than the enemy soldiers hiding in the showers in our bathroom.

In the winter when the grounds were covered with snow, I liked to wheel myself outside. If the snow was high enough I could reach over, gather a handful, and make snowballs. It was fun to throw them at my friends who were watching from their windows. Most of the time I was alone when outdoors. I had an imaginary playmate who I called Mickey and pretended was Mickey Rooney, the famous child movie star. My invisible friend and I had some good times out in the crisp winter air. However, none of them were as exciting as my attempt at flying.

*　*　*

Children in state-run institutions, including tuberculosis sanitariums, were not always treated with the kindness, compassion, and dignity that they deserved. Some were often abused by the staff. I was no exception. It is true that most of the nurses were kind and took excellent care of us. Still there were others who were not kind at all. All of the good nuns at Mercy and all of the student nurses that took care of me were the exception. They were always kind and never abusive. Ironically, while nurses who had been trained in caring for the sick were often insensitive to our needs, other hospital employees were not. Those who worked in housekeeping or as orderlies and aides were always friendly and cheered us up a great deal. Compassion is apparently something that cannot be taught, but comes from within. It is part of who you are.

I have never come to terms with the way we were often mistreated. It does not matter what their reasons may have been, no sick child away from home and family should have ever had to endure this. There was enough stress and anxiety in our young lives. We wanted our parents back. We wanted our homes and schools back. We wanted our former lives back. Often we had to wait an unreasonably long length of time when we asked for something. Perhaps it was a pillow or blanket, a bedpan, or a favorite toy that was beyond our reach. Constant verbal abuse, criticism and hurtful remarks only added to the low self-esteem many children were dealing with. Depression was a common occurrence.

Children were often punished for things that were out of their control. Some nurses would scold instead of console tearful patients who cried out at night—homesick, afraid and often in pain. We learned to tell which nurses to avoid, but it was not always possible. Sometimes we acted out because we were looking for attention, something we never got enough of. Our lives were so regimented it was no wonder we wanted a change. Change usually meant breaking the rules. We needed to find ways to break away from our neverending routine. As we got older we were afraid of what the future might hold for us. Would we be able to return to school? Would we be behind the other children our age? Would we get sick again and have to come back to the sanitarium? These questions were always on our mind.

At Homer Folks I often found it difficult to fall asleep at night. Our bedtime was very early. Night nurses warned us that there would be absolutely no talking once the door was shut for the night. Imagine a ward full of youngsters who were wide awake — children who never had a bedtime story read to them, got tucked in, or received a good-night hug or kiss at bedtime. It was the same at Biggs. Children were punished if they made too much noise at night. Needless to say we disobeyed, giggled, played our favorite games and told stories. One night while I was telling one of my popular ghost stories one of the younger children became frightened and let out a scream. A nurse stormed into the ward and wheeled his bed out into the hall without asking why he had done that. Outside of the ward there was a small alcove used to store wheelchairs and stretchers. She shoved his bed into this alcove. It was a dark, unfamiliar place, and she left him there all night. In the morning, when he was returned to the ward, he was still frightened. His voice trembled as he told us how dark it was out there and that he had been unable to sleep. He was afraid that they would not ever bring him back into the ward. Like all of us, he felt safe in the ward. Everyone still wanted me to tell ghost stories at night, but after that incident I rarely did. We were all lost children.

* * *

Every time I was moved to a private room without warning I never understood why I had to be there. Being alone in one of these rooms brought back unpleasant memories and I did not want to leave the ward. Generally no one had prepared me for these moves or told me why they were necessary.

How long will I be away from my friends on the ward?

Why did they move me here?

What is going to happen now?

Depression can have a disturbing effect on children. It was not until the 1970s that childhood depression was recognized. Psychiatrists and psychologists accepted the theory that this depression resulted from the worry, stress, anxiety, feelings of sadness and helplessness of children. When changes were made or procedures performed without any explanation I would go into a state of depression. Was I invisible? Whenever I became depressed I lost what little appetite I had. Nightmares and night terrors disturbed the sleep I needed. It was the same every time. When it was time to have my cast cut off I was never told ahead of time so that I could prepare myself mentally for this. My bed was wheeled into a private room. It was a terrifying experience to have the cast removed. The small knife or special shears that were used often cut into my skin. Once they removed the top portion of my cast they were able to wash the part of my body that had been covered for months at a time. That was the only pleasant part of this move, and I looked forward to it. When my bath was over the top of the cast was put back on and held tight with wide canvas straps. Now I could no longer turn around in bed or use a wheelchair and needed more nursing care. I remained depressed during the weeks it took before a new cast was applied and I was returned to the ward.

One of the worst experiences I had was the abuse I endured shortly after having been moved to one of these private rooms. One morning when I refused to eat, the charge nurse, who reminded me of one of the witches Elena used to tell us about, decided that the door to my room would be closed for the whole day. She placed my books on my nightstand where I could not reach them. I could not understand why she was doing this. It certainly was not my fault that I could not eat or that food often made me nauseous.

Looking out at the constant flow of traffic outside of my door, and having people occasionally stop in and visit me, were the only things that made my isolation bearable. My door was my window to the outside world, and my books were my escape from the world I found myself in. Within a few hours I started running a fever. When a doctor came in to examine me he was appalled at what had happened. He placed my books where I could reach them and comforted me. He left my door open as he stormed out angrily and apprehended the charge nurse who had given the order that my door was to be closed for the day. She never did that again, regardless of whether I ate or not. After about a week a new cast was applied and I was returned to the ward.

There were so many instances in which I was not treated fairly and I have tried to put them out of my mind. It was not until I became an adult, and especially after becoming a mother, that I started to look back and recall things that happened to me and to the other children. It is difficult for me even today to put all of this into words. I have never really come to terms with why we were treated so unkindly. There are many traits in my personality that no doubt resulted from these experiences. I like to have control of just about everything in my life. Because of this, I resent authority and being told what to do. This is especially true if I feel that the request is unreasonable. When dealing with health professionals I find myself questioning medical decisions involving not only myself but my family as well. I have no tolerance for what I consider rude behavior from those whose help I seek in our medical or surgical care regardless of the situation. Fortunately this has been an extremely rare occurrence in my life. When I entered the health care field I made it a point to treat every patient with respect, and sometimes added a little humor to cheer them up. Physicians, surgeons, physical therapists, and other medical professionals who have taken such good care of me and my family have always been treated with the respect they deserve.

Adults need to take charge of their own health care. Those who have children, those with elderly parents, and those who are caregivers need to carefully oversee every detail of their health care. One cannot afford to leave it all up to their doctors. Doctors need to be more aware of the mental health care of their patients, which is so often overlooked.

My own parents found they were helpless in their attempts to take charge of my health care during the time I was hospitalized. They became frustrated during the constant meetings they had with my doctors, even when they were given information in terms that they could understand. It was so different then. Children who were abused did not let their parents know what was going on. I never said anything to mine. We did not stop to think that if we let our parents know about our care the problem could be resolved. Maybe we thought that our parents would be angry at us for antagonizing the staff. Then there was the possibility that the staff would take it out on us. I am sure that all of the parents, including mine, realized that the hospital staff, regardless of how they treated us, were in control of their children.

* * *

There were two nurses at H that I absolutely adored. One was Miss Beatrice Gledhill, and the other I knew simply as Jennie. They were like surrogate mothers to me. Miss Gledhill was a registered nurse who was assigned to all orthopedic patients. She was quite short, while Jennie must have been almost six feet tall. When they found out how fascinated I was with the war and with airplanes, and how I had attempted to fly, they decided to take me to see the movie *Air Force*. Movies were held in the main building and I had never been there to see one. Actually I had not been to a movie since I was a toddler when my father tried to stop me from running around the theater so we would not be asked to leave.

On the night of the movie they wheeled me over to the main building on the sidewalk connecting the two buildings. Once we entered the auditorium they put my wheelchair in the aisle right next to where they sat. This movie completely captivated me. I never wanted it to end. From that night on I knew that I wanted to go to more movies—which I did. I also knew that I wanted to one day become an air force pilot—which I did not. Jennie played her harmonica on the way back. We laughed and sang as they pushed me back to H and into my room. After this first trip they continued to take me to the movies at least once a month.

Both Miss Gledhill and Jennie were so good to me, and they did it on their own time while off duty. These two remarkable women made me feel so much better about myself. They made me happy. They made me feel special.

* * *

My mother passed away in 1980. Several years later I came across an interesting four-page letter that Jennie had written to her. They had become friends, and Jennie made it a point to stop in my room when my mother was there. This letter was dated 1959. I would have liked to answer it but there was no return address. Jennie would have been in her seventies by then. Here is what she wrote:

> I guess you remember how things were run in H Bldg. until I took over and won the confidence of the children. They had been neglected. To me they were very precious. I sometimes think back and almost always it is the children I remember best. Sometime ago I was at Biggs and had a chance to go through H. It was a terrible disappointment. Rooms and hallways were stacked full of supplies. I don't get the feeling of Biggs at all when I go there. It is completely changed. I poked around there while they were rebuilding it and I just felt sick to see the destruction of what I was so familiar with. Believe me, when I left Biggs, I missed the children. I had hoped to keep in touch with all of them but the years seem to make one lose track of people.

In this letter Jennie asked about me and told my mother about some of the children she had managed to contact.

* * *

We always had a class of student nurses training at Biggs. They stayed with us for about three months and lived in the nearby nurses' dormitory. Their uniforms were more colorful than the other nurses, and they were much younger and more energetic. It was so much fun having them help take care of us. More importantly they were interested in us, what we liked, where our homes were, and what we were going to do when we returned there. When they had time they read to us and joined us in games. My favorite student nurse reminded me of Sister Mary Margaret. She loved to imitate us or members of the staff. Her best impersonation was of the charge nurse, another one of Elena's witches. After grabbing one of the children's crutches she could pretend it was a broom and prance around the room warning us of the terrible things that would happen to us if we did not do what she said.

There were many different doctors taking care of us. Some were orthopedics, doctors who specialize in the care and treatment of bovine tuberculosis. Doctors' visits were usually quite brief and we never got to know them as well as the rest of the staff. Ever since the attack on Pearl Harbor I thought that everyone who was Japanese was a Jap. Those were the people that I was so afraid would harm anyone they did not like. So you can imagine my shock one day when a young Japanese doctor, whose name I do not recall, walked into my room. He walked right over to my bed, and I cringed when he reached out to shake my hand and told me he was my new doctor.

This cannot be. Where did he come from?

Did he come to Biggs by plane?

Is he going to hurt me?

My first instinct was to ring my call bell for help. Instead I looked directly into his strange-looking eyes and asked him if he was a real Jap. I am sure my question took him by surprise, but he put me at ease by explaining that his grandparents were born in Japan but that his parents were American citizens. They had been born in the United States.

Still quite nervous, and not at all convinced that I was safe, I asked him why he bombed Pearl Harbor. He started to laugh as he explained to me that the Japanese Americans had nothing to do with that. In fact, he himself had served as a pilot in the American air force. He utterly fascinated me with his stories of being in the military and about his escapades as a boy. From that day on he was my favorite doctor — and a real pilot as well!

* * *

A year later the same supportive treatment was being used. My parents still could not understand why I was not getting any better. This time they made an appointment with Dr. Severson on one of his monthly visits. He told them that, even though I had been hospitalized for more than seven years, my current x-rays revealed a definite progression of the disease. This was not a good sign. There was extensive degeneration of the femur. Under normal circumstances this bone, located between the pelvis and knee, was the largest and strongest bone in the body. In my case there was almost complete destruction of the head and neck of the bone.

My parents were still not satisfied with my treatment and asked if there was any type of surgery that could be done. Dr. Severson explained that children with tuberculosis of the bone rarely have early surgery. This was because of the importance of preserving motion and the length of the extremity. He was hoping that with the passage of time a fusion would take place. If that were to happen I would be able to bear weight on my left leg.

Another problem that had recently developed was the formation of localized cold abscesses. A cold abscess is one that commonly accompanies tuberculosis. These abscesses develop so slowly that there is little inflammation. When there is pressure on the surrounding area they can be quite painful. In my case they were non-operable because of my condition.

Even though my hip had lost much of its motion, my condition was still not improving. Surgery was not an option.

Despite my illness, I was remarkably active and otherwise quite healthy. I had not been exposed to any of the usual childhood diseases. Staff members tried to keep me from bearing weight on my left leg but I did not listen. They were worried about the possibility of the left side pushing my entire femur through my pelvis.

Both of my parents were still working hard, struggling to pay their bills. Now that I was feeling better, despite what my doctor had told them, I noticed that they seemed to be quite tense when they came to see me. This particular summer while we were having a picnic outdoors I could not help but notice their constant arguing. It made me nervous and I thought that something terrible was going to happen. Maybe I had done something to upset them, or perhaps they were tired of visiting me every Sunday. After all, many of my friends had no company on Sunday, or even on other days. Suddenly on one visit this all changed. They told me they had some exciting news for me. Soon I would be having either a baby brother or a baby sister. Naturally I was very excited when they told me this, and very happy that they were no longer arguing on their visits.

My sister Maryann was born in the fall. She was nine years younger

Anxiously awaiting the arrival of my baby sister, Maryann, outside of Biggs in 1941. I have never seen her, although she is now ten months old. Our parents are bringing a picnic lunch.

than I. Shortly after her birth my mother became quite ill with pleurisy. She was not able to visit me for several months. Although I missed her so much, I was fortunate in having many aunts and uncles who came with my father on visiting days. When Maryann was six months old they brought me a large framed colored photograph of her. She was so beautiful, with jet black hair and an adorable smile. Everyone that came into my room admired her picture.

It was not until the following summer that I saw my sister for the first time. My parents let me hold her in my arms. She was so soft and cuddly and I never wanted to let go. Every Sunday in the summer my parents brought a picnic lunch, and I would have two whole hours with my sister. It was never enough. Once fall arrived and the weather changed they were unable to bring her to see me. When they brought her the following summer she was walking and running, no longer a baby. She no longer wanted to sit on my lap. I had missed so much.

Another family member, my mother's youngest sister Margaret, had pulmonary tuberculosis and was quite ill. She had been sick for a long time but refused to leave her husband and two young sons to enter a sanitarium. Finally she became so weak she had no choice. Aunt Margaret was admitted to the main building at Biggs. Members of my mother's family now combined their visits to see both of us. My god-parents, my mother's sister Mary and her husband Uncle Jerry, visited us both several times a week.

One day when Aunt Margaret was doing poorly, my Aunt Mary took a bus from Seneca Falls to visit her. She brought with her a chocolate cake, her sister's favorite. It was a long walk from the main road on top of the hill where the bus driver let her off. When she got to her sister's room she knew something was wrong. The door was closed, and a nurse ran down the hall to greet her. Aunt Margaret had just passed away. She was just twenty-three years old.

The Main Building

It had happened so gradually that no one really noticed, but the patient census at H kept going down. A decision had been made to close this building gradually. There had been a dramatic decrease in the number of patients with tuberculosis of the bones and joints. As most of these patients were discharged there were very few new patients admitted. It was a great shock to all of us to learn that we were going to leave H and be transferred to the main building. It would be a traumatic change for all of us, especially the children. Now that I was ten years old, I thought that my next move would be to my home.

Like most of us who lived in institutions for many years, I was completely adjusted to sanitarium life. I felt safe there. After I became familiar with the surroundings and the staff at H, I did not want to be moved again. Now I had so many friends. We were a family, and I was not sure if they would still be with me in the new building. When we were all told that there would be so many more activities there I began to feel better about the move. What I really got excited about was knowing that now I would be able to go to the movies more often.

Despite our anxiety, the move went very smoothly. It had been carefully planned for several months, and it took several weeks to complete. Large trucks were used to bring everyone and everything to our new home. This time I was not afraid, remembering Peter's kind words on the last transfer. "Today you are going on a great adventure."

All of my belongings were packed in boxes and placed on the truck with me. Clutched in one hand was the cup of colored pebbles Peter the Great had given his princess.

Although I had not realized it when I was first admitted to the main building, it was much larger than H. It was spread out on different levels of gently sloping hills. In the center there were many floors, including the surgical unit at the very top. Three two-story extensions were connected to the center. Each floor consisted of a different ward and was identified by a letter just as the children's building was. C-1 and C-2 were where all new admissions and surgical patients were housed. Women and children were placed on D-1 and D-2, and the men on E-1 and E-2. These wards were very long and measured one-eighth of a mile from end to end. All of them were identical and contained many different types of rooms. There were single and double rooms as well as rooms that could accommodate four beds. These rooms were called porch rooms because there were windows covering the entire length of one wall. At the very end of each ward there was a larger room with windows on three sides. My guess is that these very bright rooms were originally intended as a lounge area, but with the closure of H extra bed space was needed. Patients who were placed there enjoyed a spectacular panoramic view of the campus, the woods, and the lake. A nurses' station and small dining room were located in the center of the ward.

Because of the length of the ward, some rooms were quite a distance from this station. This proved to be an advantage to those adventurous souls who took great pleasure in breaking the rules. Soon after Elena was transferred to a ward she immediately started calling the nurses' station the *lookout,* and the nurses became *guards.* Of course the head nurse became the *warden.*

D-1 was located on the ground floor and overlooked the woods and lake. This was where I was relocated, along with the other children, girls and boys, and ambulatory women. Patients who were considered contagious were not admitted to this floor. Just before H closed many of the women and children were either discharged or transferred to a sanitarium closer to their homes. I never saw Jerry or Francis again, although Elena and Jean were also on D-1.

Everything was so different in this building. At H, with the exception of Jerry and Elena, we were separated from the adults. Here we found ourselves living with and interacting with grown-ups every day. As the number of children continued to decrease, I spent most of my time with them.

We no longer had a dayroom filled with dolls and toys. There were no more indoor picnics, parties, or birthday celebrations for us. We had no classroom or playground. There were many more things to do here, as we had been told, but there were few that children could take part in. Most of the children were very unhappy on this ward, but I was beginning to find out that there were actually many things to do.

My "Small Fry" column was still included in the hospital paper, even though H building was closed and many of the children had been discharged. According to this paper I was apparently the only child who preferred being in the main building. In the first issue, shortly after leaving H, I wrote "This is Small Fry saying hello from D-1 instead of H Building. All of the Small Fry like it here, but liked it better over at H. Gloria Didio goes to OT now and the movies and is very happy about it. She seems to be the happiest of the Small Fry about coming to the Main Building."

When I found out I was no longer allowed to have a radio I was really upset. Radios were not allowed because the noise might bother other patients. Instead we were given headsets that were plugged into the wall near our beds. These were connected to several radio stations. In the beginning I did not like them, but eventually I got used to them and used them all of the time. My favorite comedy shows starred Jack Benny, Bob Hope, and Edgar Bergen. Polls were taken by the hospital Radio Committee to see what shows most patients preferred. *Hollywood Star Playhouse* was the favorite with most, but not with me. I preferred *Dragnet* and the *Lone Ranger*. We were also hooked up to a radio broadcasting station that was run by the patients. There was a small studio behind the stage of the auditorium. On Sundays the *Sunday Serenade Show* offered both classical and religious music. On weekdays the *Musical Caravan* broadcast featured popular music. Once a week I enjoyed taking part as the radio announcer for a segment aired for the children. This included the things that I still wrote about in my "Small Fry" column. Sometimes I reviewed the latest children's books available in our library.

Patients on D-1 needed even less care than those in H. There were even fewer staff members on this ward. Those who were assigned there spent most of their time caring for the children and orthopedic patients.

My first room was a porch room, and I loved it because of all the windows. Jean and I were roommates again and had the whole room to ourselves. She was still in her body cast and confined to her bed, although the frame was removed. In order to let her in on all of the latest news and gossip, I always reported back to her about everything and everyone. Sometimes I would exaggerate stories to make her laugh, something that she rarely did. I am not sure she believed everything I told her, but she never let on. Jean was such a sweet girl and never complained about anything. I am not sure if I could have handled her situation as well as she did.

This floor had even less supervision and fewer rules than H. A good example of that turned into a very frightening experience for me. Soon after moving here a new cast was applied. A floor-heating lamp was placed at the end of my bed. Covers that had been rolled to the bottom of my bed caught on fire. While laying there terrified and unable to move I started screaming. A nurse in the next room quickly ran to my aid and extinguished the flames. From that day on, regardless of the fact that I was not harmed, these lamps were not used again.

Shortly after my cast was completely dry I was given another wheelchair. Each day I began to wheel myself further and further away from my room. No one seemed to notice as I started leaving the ward for longer periods of time. Since the only time I needed to be in my room was for meals and mandatory morning and afternoon naps, I had plenty of time to explore. There was so much more to see in this huge building, with the exception of the patient and surgical wards. They were off-limits. No one seemed to notice my absence, and if they did nothing was ever said.

Two elevators on different levels of the building gave me access to every floor. At H I had managed the elevator quite well, so it was no problem here. It was not long before everyone got used to seeing me — a tiny girl in pigtails — racing up and down the halls.

It did not take me long to find the section of the hospital everyone called Main Street. It was located in the center of the hospital and extended the full length of this section. There were always a lot of people and activity there and so much to see and do. It soon became my favorite place to explore and hang out. Usually I only ventured off the ward during the day. At night I was so bored and restless I decided to take a chance in the evening and go to the day room next to the auditorium. That was where the ambulatory patients, women from my ward and men from the ward across from ours (E-1) gathered every night to socialize. No one noticed or tried to stop me as I wheeled past the nurses' station. When I went to the day room the first time I worried that the adults would not want me there. Well, I did not need to worry. They invited me to play games with them and seemed to enjoy my company — as I did theirs. My favorite game was Chinese checkers and I often won, beating the very people who had taught me the game. Perhaps they let me win. Canasta was the fascinating card game everyone was playing, and they taught me how to play. Some patients brought their musical instruments, guitars and banjos, and performed for us. If someone knew how to play the piano we gathered around it and sang.

Right next door, the poolroom was a favorite gathering place for the men. There was a huge pool table and bright yellow leather couches. Only the men played pool, and I could not understand why. My father was an excellent pool player. Sometimes when he came to visit he enjoyed playing pool with the men. Patients were fascinated with his skills in this game, and he often spent time teaching them the game or how to improve their skills.

There were two large rooms for occupational therapy and two libraries. One library was for the doctors and nurses only. It contained medical and reference books as well as medical journals. Even if I could have gone in it did not interest me. I was too young. The other one was for the patients and was well stocked with all kinds of books, magazines and newspapers. There was a special section containing books for children, and I think I must have read all of them during the time I spent at Biggs. Louisa May Alcott's *Little Women*, *Little Men*, and *Jo's Boys*, along with Mark Twain's *Adventures of Tom Sawyer*, and Robert Louis Stevenson's *Treasure Island*, were among my favorites. My own collection included classics such as *The Secret Garden*, *Heidi*, *Anne of Green Gables*, and *Black Beauty*. Sometimes I read them again and again. I often read them to the other children. Both libraries contained oriental rugs, dark mahogany furniture, leather chairs and paintings with ornate frames on the walls. It was the same décor that had been in H building. When I was between casts and unable to get to the library, the librarian brought a cart full of books to my room just as she had when I was first admitted there. Grandpa Giovannini made me a small bookcase to store my books in.

During the day a small store was open where you could buy snacks, sodas, gifts, newspapers and magazines. It also served as a post office. This store was always busy, but I had trouble moving my wheelchair in there because the store was so small. When the clerks saw me coming they knew exactly what kind of soda and candy bar to get out for me. At last I started gaining some weight. Jean loved it when I brought treats back for her as well.

A lobby and auditorium faced the end of this busy area. One day as I was wheeling by the auditorium, I heard someone playing the piano. When I opened the door there was my friend Warren, whom I never thought I would see again, practicing his music lesson on a baby grand piano. He seemed very happy to see me; perhaps living on the complex was as lonely as being there as a patient. When he asked me what I was doing there, I told him about the move from H to the main building and of still having Jean as a roommate. Warren and his friend Deagan had figured that I had been transferred to a different sanitarium.

We spent time reminiscing about his visits to H when he had performed tricks on his bicycle and flown his kite to entertain me. Warren told me that he came there almost every day to practice. From then on I saw him several times a week. Since I was not sure how the staff would feel about this, I was careful not to mention it to anyone except Jean.

While wandering around on the bottom floor I heard voices and laughter. It was coming through the double doors leading into the main dining room. I looked in and saw the ambulatory men and women sitting at round tables beautifully set with white linens. This room, like so many of the rooms there, was elegantly furnished. It looked and sounded so festive, and how I wished that I could have my meals in there as well. I could also hear the sounds coming from the kitchen which was located behind the dining room.

One floor that I will never forget was the one where all of the diagnostic testing took place. How I dreaded it when I was taken to the clinical laboratory there, where periodically technicians drew my blood for testing. It always hurt, and I usually created quite a scene trying to prevent them from sticking needle after needle into my tiny veins. There was an unpleasant smell coming from the chemicals that were used in that room. In order to be sure that my lungs were clear, especially since I was often unknowingly exposed to patients who were contagious, I had to have my sputum tested. Since I had no sputum to bring up all that went into the cup was spit. I think they eventually became tired of trying to grow something in that. So instead they collected my gastric fluid for analysis. This was even more painful and unpleasant than the blood draw. It was really disgusting. In this procedure I was given pieces of ice to chew on while a technician inserted a thin rubber tube through my nose and into my stomach. A syringe was used to withdraw gastric contents to be examined for tubercle bacilli. They never found any, but they never gave up trying.

Radiology was located right across the hall from the laboratory. Whenever my cast was removed, I was taken to the room where x-rays were taken and put on a very hard table. The table was very cold and I had to lie on it for a long time while the technician took the pictures. Once he was done I had to remain there until he checked the results.

Sometimes the pictures had to be taken many times. It was easier for them to have me stay in this position in case the pictures had to be repeated. It seemed like I was there for hours, alone and uncomfortable with nothing to do. To pass the time I either counted all of the tiles on the ceiling, or just closed my eyes and flew over rooftops. That was how I got through it. As usual no one came in to talk to me or to explain anything. After all, I suppose I was just another patient on a never-ending assembly line of lost children.

At the end of the hall, just outside of the diagnostic area, there were tables with large jars on them. They contained specimens of diseased lungs and parts of lungs in glass containers. This did not make any more sense to me than the creatures with gaping holes in their side at H, yet they were also part of medical research. The specimens were even more disgusting than the snake-like tubing they slid down my throat.

*　　*　　*

There were not as many children in wheelchairs in the main building. Although the few that were there were not as daring as I was and never left the ward, we all loved to play wheelchair games. We called ourselves the Wheelchair Brigade. Some adults thought we were too noisy and were not amused by our antics. I am sure they prayed that our Brigade would be impounded by the staff. Others loved to watch us, often cheering us on as we passed their rooms.

One of our favorite games was called Crash. Two of us would wheel our chairs to opposite ends of the long corridors, turn around and face each other, and race towards one another as fast as we could. Just as we were about to run into each other we would quickly turn our chairs back to back — and crash. Although I do not remember anyone ever falling out of their chair, I do remember that we really trashed some of them. Sometimes we put things in the spokes of the wheels, producing eerie sounds as we sped down the halls. Playing catch was a favorite with most, but not with me. I was terrible at throwing and catching a ball. As one who was very competitive, I had no interest in participating in games I did not do well in.

Occasionally I used my chair as a scooter. First I would carefully push myself into an upright position. This was no easy task with a cast on. Then I somehow managed to stand up, turn around, place my right foot on the floor and glide off. Once I gathered enough speed I placed my foot on the footrest and enjoyed the ride. It is no wonder that I ruined so many casts.

Education in the main building was quite different than it had been at H. With so few children to teach, it was not necessary to have a regular classroom or to hire a teacher. Our teachers were patients who had teaching degrees. If there were more than two children at the same grade level their classes were held in one of the porch rooms. For single students a teacher would go to their rooms. Sometimes we had qualified teachers who were not ambulatory. They were still in the contagious stage of their disease. Students had to go to them. Those of us with bone tuberculosis could not go to their room for class. Our education was very sporadic. There was constant change as new admissions and discharges took place. When I told my teachers that I had often taught younger students at Homer Folks they let me do the same.

There were eleven students in grades one through eight and we took basic subjects that included reading, writing, English, geography and arithmetic. Eight students were in high school. They were taught English, social studies, languages, history and mathematics. There were no classes in science or labs. Shorthand and typing were offered as extra subjects that one day might prove useful in seeking employment. Correspondence courses for high school graduates were available through the International Correspondence School.

It was crucial for all of us not to fall behind our peers while hospitalized, and we had the satisfaction of knowing we were not missing all of our courses while at Biggs. Students worked at their own pace and took examinations when their teacher felt they were ready. One could advance from grade to grade without following a regular school year. There was no time off from study during the summer. No one seemed to mind because it gave us something to do.

My first communion took place in my room at Biggs in 1940. Although my cast is partially hidden by my dress, I am able to kneel on just one leg by placing the one in a cast over the side of the bed.

Once discharged many were able to return to their former schools, and often were able to be in their original class. This did not apply to me since I had only attended kindergarten for a short time, and my parents had moved to Seneca Falls.

There was no religious education. Catholic and Protestant services were held every Sunday in either the auditorium or a day room. I had been told by my parents that we were Catholics, but I had no idea of what that meant. They were anxious to have me make my first communion and start attending mass. A priest from Ithaca came to Biggs once a week to conduct mass. Arrangements were made to have him prepare me for this religious sacrament. At Mercy the nuns had already taught me many of the simple prayers, so even though I did not understand what they meant, I knew they were something special. This surely had to be something special as well.

When this priest came to my room for the first time I found I was not at all comfortable with him. Perhaps it was because of the black pants and shirt with the tiny white neckline. He looked like a warlock. He was kind enough, but told me the strangest things that I could not understand. To add to my confusion he said that it was time to prepare for my first confession. I asked him what that meant. He explained that I would have to tell him about all of the sins I had ever committed and gave examples, such as telling lies. Because I was afraid of what he might say or do if I told him what "sins," I had, perhaps I would just tell him I did not have any. They certainly were none of his business. For weeks I thought about what I would tell him. I wondered if my sins consisted of hiding hot cereal under the top lid of my nightstand, or peeking at my friend Francis's private parts? Or maybe I had sinned by talking too loud at bedtime or sticking my tongue out at a nurse who seemed to delight in braiding my hair so tight I thought it would fall out?

I asked him what his name was and he said to call him father. Why? He was not my father. He tried to explain to me that if I told him my sins and said a few prayers all of my sins would disappear. Well, I thought, was he some kind of a magician? I did not believe he could make things disappear but, if he could, I wished he could make my sickness disappear as well.

On the day he came to my room to hear my confession, I simply told him some things my parents had suggested. They knew more about my sins than I did. Apparently he seemed satisfied and had me say just two short prayers. They were the same ones the nuns at Mercy had taught me years ago.

Family and friends, all dedicated Catholics, were always bringing me religious articles. I am sure they thought that these would help in my recovery. There were statues, crosses, and rosary beads. You were supposed to say a prayer on each bead. It took a long time with the beads, and I did not always finish. At night, once the lights were turned off, I managed to turn myself over on my stomach. Then I lifted myself up on my elbows and carefully arranged my favorite religious pieces in a semicircle on my bed. Baby Jesus in his tiny crib was always in the center. As I touched each one I said a little prayer, asking God to please make me well so that I could walk again and go home. Surely if the priest could make my sins disappear, God could do the same with my illness.

This little ritual went on for months, but eventually I became discouraged and stopped. Apparently God had not heard me. I wondered where he was and whether he was in heaven, as the priest had said, or everywhere. If he was everywhere he must know about children who are sick, who cannot walk, children who cried out in pain during the night. Maybe he really did not exist at all.

My parents were more excited about my first communion than I was. They bought me a beautiful white dress which fit over my cast. There was a matching white veil. Wearing it made me feel like a princess. Many members of my family came for this special occasion. If only Peter and Sister Mary Margaret had been there to see me. Once the priest gave me my communion he distributed it to everyone who was in the room with me. I knelt at the end of my bed on my good knee while the leg in the full cast hung over the side. My parents took many pictures of me that day. This was unusual because pictures of me were rarely taken. Perhaps they did not own a camera.

Every Sunday morning after that I wheeled myself to wherever mass was being held. Masses were said in Latin, and I did not understand anything that was going on. Shortly after my first communion I started losing interest and stopped attending. One Sunday morning while roaming the halls I heard people singing in the day room. Someone was playing the piano. When I went in I found a Protestant service being held. These services were in English, and the songs were called hymns. Everyone had a book with the songs in it. They sounded so beautiful, and there were so many of them. Often on Sundays after that I stopped in to listen to the music. Sometimes when I was in the auditorium alone I tried to pick out some of the hymns on the piano.

It was while listening to music on my headphones that I discovered the engaging voice of Frank Sinatra. He was a new young singer who was rapidly becoming famous. Along with thousands of other young girls, I became completely obsessed with him. Soon I was one of the thousands of fans who were called "bobby soxers," even though this fan wore a sock on just one foot.

It was time to put away my miniature army and bedside rifle. Comic books were replaced with movie magazines. I cut out every picture and story about my Frankie and pasted them into scrapbooks. My parents got permission to bring me a small phonograph, and soon I had a collection of every one of his records. Even though I could not join his fans as they flocked to theaters, gathering outside of his stage door screaming and swooning just at the sight — or sound — of him, I was just as carried away as they were. One day, while listening to him sing my favorite song, "Night and Day," I unintentionally let out a scream that sent several nurses running into my room. They were student nurses and were as mesmerized with this young man as I was, although they were not allowed to wear bobby sox to work.

My grandparents from Seneca Falls surprised me on my eleventh birthday with a small replica of a baby grand piano. It had real keys that worked, a top that lifted up, and was perfect for playing my favorite songs while using just one finger. One day I hoped to play a real piano like the one Warren used.

One morning while listening to Warren play the piano I noticed that he was unusually quiet. When I asked him if there was anything wrong he stopped practicing his lesson and told me that this would be the last time we would see each other. His father had taken a job at another hospital very far from Biggs. Tears filled my eyes as Warren stood up, bent down towards me, and kissed me. He held me tight as we said our last goodbye. Like so many others I had become attached to, I never saw him again.

Several weeks later when I went into the auditorium there was a young man there playing the piano. He was much better at it than Warren. He told me that his name was David and that he was also a patient. Recently he had been admitted to E-1 and was given permission to use the piano. When he discovered my interest in music he told me he had stacks of sheet music and books and had played in a small orchestra before he became ill. We started meeting in there nearly every day and he played all kinds of music for me. He tried to give me lessons, but it was difficult because of the slanted position I was in because of my cast. Still we managed to play simple duets. Learning how to really play the piano was another thing I added to the growing list of things I wanted to do once I was discharged.

Biggs offered all kinds of entertainment that took place on the stage in the auditorium. Movies were held once a week and some form of live entertainment took place several times a month. There were variety and minstrel shows, magicians, hypnotists, puppets and ventriloquists. Community groups that provided wonderful shows for us included the Ithaca Community Players and Rotary club. We were fortunate in being located near Ithaca, an educational community and home of Ithaca College, where David had studied music, and Cornell University. Students from their Departments of Music and Theater Arts provided us with a variety of outstanding productions. There were concerts with full orchestras, music ensembles, choral groups, soloists, and plays. One evening a young female music student who played the harp appeared as a soloist with one of the orchestras. This was an instrument I had never seen or heard before and I was completely captivated by its haunting sounds.

Sometimes when professional entertainers performed at the colleges they came to Biggs to perform for us. Paul Robeson, who was famous all over the world as a singer, actor and activist, graciously honored us with a visit and recital. His exceptional performance was a source of inspiration to all of us who were lucky enough to hear him. I will never forget his deep baritone voice in his powerful rendition of the classic favorite, "Old Man River."

World War II had a serious impact on us. We were dealing with our own private war on tuberculosis and did not need another battle. Some staff members joined the armed forces so there were now fewer people to take care of us. Gasoline rationing had an effect on the number of visitors we had. Fewer outside visits created stress. Car sharing helped, but only in a very small way. There were time conflicts, and families and friends were scattered throughout the area. My parents somehow still managed to make their weekly visit. Our relatives helped by letting them use their rationed gas, or even their cars.

Most of the patients were unbelievable in their determination to do what they could to assist in the war effort. This included full cooperation with the hard-pressed hospital staff. Letters were sent to loved ones serving their countries. In my letters to Uncle Aldo, who was now stationed in Italy, I added little poems and words of encouragement.

> Dear Uncle Aldo,
> When you get back home you can come and visit me
> and we will go outside and you can push me real fast up
> and down the hills ... maybe we could have a picnic.
> Stay safe and come home soon.
> Kill the Germans. Send them to the moon.
> Love, Gloria

Now that there were fewer visitors, something had to be done in the additional free time most patients had. An Entertainment Committee was formed to search for patients and staff members who were willing to take part in providing entertainment. We were all quite surprised that there was so much untapped talent among us. We had singers, actors, and musicians who played the piano, guitar, and even banjo. Others organized and coordinated a variety of events. A Biggs Little Theater Group was formed, and many of the plays that were presented were written by patients. Everyone was encouraged to look into and contact any school or community group willing to perform for us. Our in-house radio station was the venue for a new group — the Biggs Mighty Workshop Players. Patients read plays over the air and held panel discussions on topics they felt would be of interest to listeners.

As much as everyone was upset about the war, it seemed to have a positive effect on the patients. Being so involved in helping out took their minds off their own battle, and made them more determined than ever to get well.

Patients also helped in the war effort by setting up a war savings program. There were contests with prizes for those who either sold or purchased the largest number of war bonds or stamps.

A lot of information about the war appeared in the hospital paper, the *Tower News*. Patients were encouraged to submit stories and articles about the war and about friends and family members who were serving their country. Each issue still contained current news at Biggs as well as lists of admissions and discharges, birthdays, movies and other entertainment. Our doctors continued to write medical articles, many of which I have gleaned information from for my story. They answered questions about tuberculosis and brought everyone up to date on the latest advances in treatment.

In reporting the news of their fellow patients on the wards the women reporters gave interesting and friendly coverage. They tried to include everyone in their columns. Male reporters, on the other hand, were merciless in what they wrote. They reported the names of those who kept their roommates awake with their loud snoring or went outside to smoke. It was all done with humor, and they had a tendency to exaggerate. They let us know who was putting on weight, who had become reclusive, and who was having luck with the ladies. I am sure their columns were everyone's favorites — except members of the staff who did not see the humor in reading about their escapades. Sometimes I think these reporters wrote about events that were either exaggerated, or never really took place, to deliberately upset them. For many readers these reports not only made them laugh but helped reduce their ongoing stress.

Everyone, including the children, seemed to enjoy occupational therapy. Its beneficial exercise to aid recovery was prescribed and then carefully monitored by the doctors. Therapy was accomplished through making all kinds of things with the help of the therapists. All of the equipment and supplies were provided. Patients on bed rest were able to do needlework and drawing and were given instructions in their rooms. It was amusing to see male patients knitting, crocheting and tatting. They took a great deal of pride in their work and did not seem to mind the constant kidding they had to put up with.

Ambulatory patients were able to go to the occupational therapy shops. As patients advanced in their cure painting and leatherwork were added to the program. These rooms were well equipped with large weaving looms, sewing machines and typewriters. There were all kinds of tools and machines for working with leather, wood and metal. One area was used for ceramics, painting and drawing. Many patients were very talented artists, and their paintings and drawings were displayed throughout the building.

Patients took great pride in making gifts for their families and friends. Jewelry was the most popular gift made. I enjoyed making an assortment of potholders and pocketbooks for my family using the large intricate looms for weaving. They were not perfect, but I just beamed when everyone made such a fuss over them. Sometimes the items patients made were sent to the Tompkins County Fair. There they were able to sell things they had made. Often they won prizes for their handiwork.

Just before holidays and theme parties, there was a flurry of activity in the shops. Committees busied themselves making decorations. Halloween was the time everyone really got creative working with decorations and costumes. Halloween night they formed a procession and went up and down all of the wards, much to the delight of those confined to their beds. Men from E-1 loved to dress as staff nurses and ran around answering patient's bells and handing out fake bedpans and urinals. Even the staff got into the act and wore outlandish costumes. Sometimes they dressed as patients in pajamas and robes and used wheelchairs. One year I again attached cardboard airplane wings and a propeller to my wheelchair. Dressed as a pilot, goggles and all, I took first place in the children's category.

In addition to the benefit of adding exercise to their cure, occupational therapy helped people deal with the monotony of the institutions. It was a great stress reducer and was an important factor in getting well.

During the Christmas season the hospital and grounds were transformed into an enchanting holiday wonderland. At the entrance of the grounds visitors were greeted by a huge illuminated Santa and sleigh filled with gifts and drawn by six reindeer. A twelve-foot tree, brilliant with lights, stood majestically at the hospital's entrance. A large star cast its light from the roof of the tower. In the lobby, there was a wooden replica of a manger, complete with the baby Jesus. Small fir trees surrounded it, and a colorful old-fashioned Noel scene completed the display. A gigantic snowman greeted everyone at the door of the auditorium. Inside this room, as well as in the dayroom and dining room, wreaths and candles were added to the décor. Each ward had its own eight-foot Christmas tree. Lights in the corridors were covered with green and red streamers. Small branches of evergreens and pinecones adorned every patient's door. On Christmas Eve staff members walked through the corridors singing carols.

Some patients were allowed to go home for the holidays, but the majority stayed right there. During my second year on D-1 my doctors started granting us weekend passes twice a year. My first pass was for Christmas. I was so excited I counted the days, hours, and minutes until my parents arrived to take me home.

My parents were living in a small apartment that was walking distance from my grandparents. When they picked me up for the trip home they had some difficulty getting me in the back seat of the car because of my cast. They had to use a lot of pillows and position me so that I would not fall. It seemed to take forever to make this journey. I

Arriving home in 1942 on a weekend pass. I have not been home in seven years.

Top: Raking leaves from my wheelchair in 1943 while home for a few days. *Bottom:* Mom joins me on the lawn on another weekend pass in 1942. I am still in my body cast.

had not been away from Biggs in three years. When we arrived at the apartment my father put me in a wheelchair that they had borrowed from the local hospital. Everything looked so different both inside and outside of our apartment. It was nothing like the sanitarium.

My cast made it very difficult for me to get around, and my father had to carry me everywhere. All of the doorways turned out to be too narrow for the wheelchair, so he put it on the small porch next to the kitchen. When I was carried to bed I could hardly move around because the mattress was so soft. Still somehow we all managed, and the weekend went by all too quickly.

It was not the kind of Christmas that I was used to, but I loved it. There was so much activity. Visitors were constantly coming in and out. I could not believe the amount of food and drinks that were served. Maryann and I played together at home for the first time. She was now a toddler and loved running through the apartment. This first visit home was the hardest. When it was time to return to Biggs I pleaded with my parents not to take me back, saying that I hated the hospital and that I wanted to stay home forever. It did not matter about the inconveniences because of my cast, or the narrow doorways which prevented me from using a wheelchair. When they explained why this was not possible I refused to listen, and I lashed out at them, accusing them of not wanting me home.

On the way back to Biggs I was miserable and my heart sank. I thought that they did not want me to stay home, and that they did not really love me. During the seemingly endless trip back I would not talk. I never wanted the trip to end because I knew that once we got there my parents would have to leave. They were probably thinking the same thing and were saddened by the fact that bringing me home had made me not want to return to the hospital. Later when they brought me to my room and kissed me goodbye they seemed reluctant to leave.

On this first night back I felt so homesick I could not sleep and felt like I was going to be sick. Once my door was closed all I could think about was my home. As I lay there crying I hoped one of the nurses would hear me and come in to talk to me, but the nurses just ignored me. They were used to this happening following children's home visits. Desperate for their attention I deliberately started screaming. That got their attention, but even though they tried, they were unable to comfort me. Soon I was so exhausted that I fell into a deep sleep, flying over rooftops—flying home to my real family — to be one of the happy children.

It was so much better going home in the summer because I could be outside. When I was given permission for a weekend pass, I would hold my sister on my lap while someone pushed my wheelchair. She loved it. Sometimes my mother would spread a blanket on the lawn, and the two of us would color and draw. Usually one of our young uncles would join us.

Although these visits were short, they gave me some idea of what life would be like living at home. It was not as comfortable as the sanitarium, but I thrived on all of the attention and love I received. They hugged me and kissed me. I could not get enough of the feeling of someone touching me. For a very brief period I became one of the happy children. It often took days, even weeks, to get over feeling miserable. Nothing interested me and I was not myself. At night I dreamt of home, but when I woke up in the morning in my hospital bed I realized it was just a dream and how unhappy I was.

* * *

"I am in that temper that if I were under water
I would scarcely kick to come to the top."
— John Keats on depression, May 1818

It was not until the 1970s and I was well into my thirties that psychiatrists and other mental health professionals started taking a good look at the symptoms and treatment of children who suffer from depression. Feelings of sadness, hopelessness, worry and fear were common among children that had been institutionalized for years. My anxiety disorder evolved from being separated from my parents and from my distress when they had to leave. Times that I lacked an appetite and could not eat had been directly related to childhood depression and stress. There was never any counseling by mental health professionals regardless of how severe our depression was. No medications were given for this. We were not prepared for all of the changes we would have to face once we became patients. Treatments, transfers and placements had a profound effect on our mental as well as our physical health. When I was finally discharged I still had episodes of depression, but as the years went on they occurred less frequently. Finally they simply disappeared.

Extended Family

At the beginning of the twentieth century there was such a stigma to having tuberculosis that people who had it would try to hide it in an effort to avoid prejudice and hostility. Often their friends and family did the same thing. They would even pretend that the person who was ill was away, perhaps on a holiday, or that they had moved to another location, or that they had polio. My own mother was one of those people.

"Gloria," my mother had said to me shortly after I was discharged and living at home, "please do not tell anyone that you had tuberculosis."

This request was one that I have never forgotten and it took me totally by surprise. When I asked her why not, she explained that people would not understand the fact that my kind of tuberculosis was not contagious, and that they were in no danger of getting it by contact with me. She told me to tell anyone who asked that I had polio. I could not believe what she was saying, and I certainly did not want to tell people that I had polio. It made me uncomfortable. The irony of this was that it was polio that was highly contagious while skeletal tuberculosis was not.

Children look at things differently. As a child I had no idea of why people, including my own mother, were so afraid of tuberculosis. I had no knowledge of what this disease was all about. While growing up in sanitariums with constant exposure to adult patients, I gradually started to find out many things about their disease as well as my own. Throughout my life I have spent a considerable amount of time learning as much as I can about tuberculosis.

In the 1930s and early 1940s tuberculosis had changed not only my life, but the lives of millions—including my fellow patients, my family at Biggs. Pulmonary tuberculosis was the leading cause of death in the United States. Symptoms included a persistent cough, chest pain, sputum streaked with blood, weight loss, night sweats, weakness and fatigue.

Once there was an awareness that the route of transmission was from person to person the general public panicked. Fear of this disease in the United States was so widespread that desperate measures were taken to stop its spread. Boards of health were formed to both monitor and help prevent an epidemic. Children who had tuberculosis had to leave school. Adults were often forced out of hotels and boarding houses. Those with the advanced disease were unable to work. They often suffered pain in moving and breathing. Foreigners with tubercular symptoms were refused admission to the United States by the Immigration Department. We became a very phobic society. There was even an ordinance against spitting in public. In addition to the fear of spit there was also a fear of dust. This led to a great emphasis on cleanliness in the home, in the workplace, and in personal hygiene.

As the general public became aware of the fact that these bacteria were contagious, they became frightened and often hysterical as they stood by helplessly and watched their friends and family become ill and sometimes die. They realized that they too were at risk of getting the disease, which they could pass on to others, and which could be fatal. It was often referred to as the White Plague or the Captain of Death. A common name for it was consumption, as the disease literally consumed those who had it.

Many people possessed an unreasonable fear of tuberculosis. They believed that they could escape infection by shunning the known tubercular person. Actually it was the undiagnosed patients in society who posed the greatest threat. Thousands of people with active tuberculosis walked the streets every day. Some felt that their poor health was due to other reasons, and some just did not want anyone to know. Many developed a mild case and overcame it without ever knowing that they had been infected.

An uninformed public did not realize that there are actually many types of tuberculosis, and that it can attack virtually every organ of the body. Usually they identified it as the very contagious form that occurs in the lungs, as that was where it occurred most often. Skeletal tuberculosis, although not contagious, came from infected milk. In milary tuberculosis the germs spread throughout the body through the bloodstream. Patients with tuberculosis meningitis have the infection in their brain.

Insurance companies across the nation refused to sell insurance to people with the disease. A number of health and safety laws were put into effect all over the country. Laws were passed in state legislatures in an attempt to bring about control of the disease. Couples were sometimes advised not to marry or, if already married, not to sleep together or have children. There was even a big problem getting nurses to care for those who were hospitalized. Hospitals often had to operate their own nursing schools.

Everything possible was done to get rid of this deadly and rapidly spreading disease. A war to rid the country of tuberculosis was waged. It became a national obsession as panic prevailed and the disease continued to spread.

Although tuberculosis appeared in epidemic form in the nineteenth century in the United States and Europe, no one was sure what caused this dreadful life-threatening disease. Due to the crowded living and working conditions of the poor, they seemed to be the most susceptible. Yet no one, not even the wealthiest, was safe.

It was the introduction of the sanitarium cure that was the first step against tuberculosis. There were only a few of them in the United States at that time. When an American doctor, Dr. Edward Livingston Trudeau, developed tuberculosis, he went to the Adirondacks at Saranac Lake in New York State. He soon discovered that the fresh mountain air somehow lessened his symptoms, so he started a small tuberculosis colony there. In 1882 he established the Adrian Cottage Sanitarium. This was the beginning of the sanitarium movement in the United States. Like others at the time, Dr. Trudeau believed that exposure to the outdoors, regulation of daily habits, rest, and a nutritious diet would make people well.

Following Trudeau's example, other sanitariums were built in that area. With the introduction of the sanitarium the first step in the war against tuberculosis took place. A public health movement began to promote community participation, with an emphasis on a healthy lifestyle and ordinances to improve sanitation and overcrowded slum housing. Voluntary organizations to combat the disease were formed during this time and included the National Tuberculosis Association in 1904, now called the American Lung Association. This organization sells Christmas seals every year. Their mission is to prevent lung disease and to promote lung health.

Sanitariums were often established from existing structures and often resembled resorts rather than institutions. Eventually hundreds of sanitariums were built across the nation. Now people with tuberculosis could be isolated from those who did not have the disease. Many felt it was the only way to stop the epidemic. Patients in sanitariums had their daily lives regulated and controlled in an effort to speed their recovery. In this setting, it was felt they would finally be cured and eventually be released. In the 1930s there were more than six hundred sanitariums in this country. Dr. DeMarco, my doctor at Mercy Hospital, realized that the only place I would have a chance to get well was in one of them.

*   *   *

Skeletal tuberculosis caused by *Mycobacterium bovis* in infected cattle was rare after the introduction of pasteurization. Commercially pasteurized milk, which was virtually nonexistent in 1900, composed about 98 percent of the milk supply in 1936. I had been infected in 1934. Government agencies eliminated the problem of bovine tuberculosis in humans by eradicating it in livestock through the tuberculin testing of cattle and disposal of those that were infected. Nationwide surveillance programs were established. By the 1940s in the United States new cases were extremely rare.

Farmers today are devastated if they find out that one or more of their cattle have tested positive for the deadly bovine bacillus. Their farms are put under quarantine, and infected cattle are put to death in an effort to prevent an epidemic that could have an adverse effect on the livestock industry.

Despite all of the progress that was continually being made, pulmonary and extra-pulmonary tuberculosis remained a major public health concern.

*   *   *

Things had not changed much at the time of my transfer to the main building. There was still no cure, and the adults whom I would get to know had a long and difficult road ahead of them. Their average age was between twenty and forty, a young adult population. As the children's census kept going down I found myself spending more and more time with these patients. They were now my extended family, and they both enriched and influenced my life in many ways. From this diverse population Jerry had introduced me to poetry. Ana, a talented artist, gave me lessons in oil painting and watercolors. David taught me the basics of playing the piano and encouraged me to continue with it when

I returned home. A patient who spoke fluent Spanish taught me some of the language. It sounded so much like the Italian my family occasionally spoke to each other when they came to visit. A young man who had served in the military fascinated me with his stories of army life. People shared with me stories of their lives before they became ill, and what their plans were once they were discharged.

I spent so much time with the adults. They were constantly talking about their cure and their treatment, and I was becoming quite familiar with so much of what they were going through. At a very young age I knew about how doctors treated patients with pulmonary tuberculosis by collapsing their lungs. They did this through procedures called pneumothorax and thoracoplasty.

There were a few orthopedic patients on D-1 that had both pulmonary and bone tuberculosis. My friend Elena from H was one of them. This was especially disturbing because even when one form of the disease was arrested they still had the other to contend with. Since most of them had the more common tuberculosis of the spine, they were forced to remain in bed even when their pulmonary disease was arrested. It had to be an absolute nightmare for them.

Elena had again been placed in a single room. Although she had many visitors, just as she had at H, being alone in a room for such a long time had to be difficult. Everyone loved her, especially the male patients and orderlies. They could not do enough for her, and she took full advantage of them when they brought her special treats and entertained her with hilarious accounts of hospital gossip. Everyone adored this remarkable and courageous young woman who was spending her tenth year confined to her bed.

It was through talking with Elena that I began to realize what the situation was for those of us with bone tuberculosis. There were concerns about just who was taking care of us, monitoring our treatment plans. While it was true that the nurses and orderlies took care of our basic needs, many felt that the monthly visits from the orthopedic group from Syracuse were not enough. Our doctor, Dr. Severson, was a very quiet man who rarely spoke directly to us.

Prior to these monthly visits the staff made so much fuss about them that it made most patients feel quite intimidated. We were told to stay in our rooms and in our beds until they left. An entourage of nurses and doctors accompanied them on their rounds. These visits were very short and very little information was given to patients. As a result patients felt helpless, vulnerable. It seemed the doctors talked around them, as though they were invisible. For my own part I never took these monthly visits seriously, and was only annoyed because I had to remain in my room until they left.

After one of these visits I wheeled myself into Elena's room. As I entered I immediately knew that something was very wrong. She was sobbing. Her doctors had just told her that her spine was still not healing and that she would have to remain in a cast indefinitely.

As I held her hand and watched the tears flow slowly down her cheeks, I was beginning to grasp the seriousness of our situation. I was eleven years old.

Another young woman, Betty, also had spinal and pulmonary disease. She was one of the most beautiful women I had ever seen. She looked like a princess in a fairy tale with her brilliant blue eyes, fair skin, and long blonde curly hair. She had it combed upward, where it formed a cascade of ringlets and curls that made a golden halo over her pillow. Her doctors insisted that she have her hair cut but she refused. It was her way of asserting her independence. Unlike Elena she seemed quite withdrawn — one of the quiet ones. Although I stopped in her room occasionally, it was apparent that she did not want to talk to anyone. She seemed very sad, and certainly had reason to be.

A young woman, Carol, became my close friend. Carol could not have been more than nineteen years old. How I admired her. She was very outgoing and fun to be with. Although she had undergone two major surgeries on her lungs, she had a very positive attitude about her condition. She was the first one to call me Glo, which has remained my nickname. Every morning, dressed in her long bright-red bathrobe, she stopped by my room on her way to fill her water pitcher. One day she asked me if I would like to see the incisions from her surgery. When I refused she just laughed and told me she did not like looking at them either. She also told me that she would probably never want to be seen in a bathing suit. Not wanting to offend her, I finally consented to see her incisions.

When she removed her pajama top and I saw the long ugly scars on her chest I could not believe what I saw. Her chest was disfigured and appeared to be caved in. It looked much worse than I had imagined, but I lied and told her it was not so bad. She could always get one of those bathing suits that covered her chest. I have often wondered if Carol ever went swimming or sunbathing with her young friends once she returned home. Her surgical incision was the only one I had ever seen. Years later I had a better understanding of the various kinds of lung surgeries and what she had gone through.

*   *   *

Patients admitted to Biggs came from all over the state. Although there seemed to be an effort to place them as close to their homes as possible, some were still far away from home. Patients whose families lived far away had few visitors. This was especially difficult for them, as it had often been for me, during visiting hours when patients who were more fortunate had company. There was a theory that sanitariums were built in rural areas not only for the fresh air, but also as a way of limiting visitors. To my knowledge that was never proven.

Everyone's future was uncertain and everything in their lives was now secondary to the business of getting well. There was no turning back. Decisions had to be made or were made for them on careers, marriages, and even on having a family. Home treatment was an alternative to a sanitarium and was referred to as home rest cure. Some people actually lived in tents or cabins so that the fresh air inhaled would kill the deadly bacilli.

At Biggs all new admissions, as well as patients who were the sickest or having surgery, were placed on C-1 and C-2 wards. Since I did not have pulmonary tuberculosis I was never placed there. Patients referred to their treatment plan as taking the cure. Resting the diseased area was essential in the treatment of tuberculosis. New admissions were put on complete bed rest. This meant they could not even get up to use the bathroom or take showers. There were no curative drugs at the time, but other medicines were administered to promote rest and improve their general condition. Doctors had to be careful in treating this chronic disease. Every effort was made not to use habit-forming narcotic drugs. Medicines were used for symptoms such as pain in the pleural area, cough, insomnia and fever. A complete medical examination and evaluation with special attention to the chest was very important. After that the diagnostic workups began. This was done with stethoscopes, x-rays, laboratory testing of sputum and body fluids, and a tuberculin test. Once all of this was accomplished doctors were able to prescribe their course of treatment.

Institutional life was not easy. New patients soon found that they had to make adjustments physically, mentally and emotionally. Physically this meant staying right in bed all of the time. Mentally it meant using your mind to aid in your cure. Body rest was of little value without mental rest. Two forces were at war with one another: acceptance vs. denial. Stress due to anxiety, frustration, worry and depression were the enemy of the cure. Emotionally it meant you were taken from your home environment and placed in a place where rules and regulations came ahead of personal desires.

It took courage and determination to make these adjustments. There were strict schedules and rigid routines to follow. Some dealt with this better than others. Organized rest cures were monotonous and left patients with too much time on their hands—too much time to think about the past and worry about what the future held for them. Tuberculosis became a battle of the mind as well as of the body, a battle which often took years to win. During that time they could have setbacks. After discharge they could have a recurrence. In the back of everyone's minds was the knowledge that they might even die.

Those in denial often agonized over lost opportunities. Worried and frightened about their health, they were sure they would not win this battle. They had a hard time adjusting and usually kept to themselves in a self-imposed isolation. On the positive side they seemed more serious about obeying the rules, although some left against medical advice. Others took little interest in the activities that were available or in socializing with their fellow patients.

Life was much easier for those who accepted their fate. They were able to adjust to the structured routine and monotony of their lives. These patients interacted with their fellow patients and the staff, and took advantage of all of the programs and numerous things there were for them to do. Positive attitudes played an important part in their cure. Humor was often used as a coping mechanism, and there were constant pranks played on one another and on the staff.

There was often bitterness towards the staff because patients felt that they did not communicate enough with them about their illness. This made some of them feel like they were being treated like children. Sometimes new admissions were members of the staff themselves who got the disease. Even though they took the necessary precautions, it seemed as though no one was safe. Often there were members of the same family hospitalized. Usually they were on different floors due either to gender or the stage of their cure. One young mother told me how much she enjoyed getting mail from her son. He was on a different ward and sent her cartoons that he had drawn for her.

Death for those with the advanced form of the disease was often painful. There was difficulty in breathing, eating, and even talking. Eventually I got used to the sound of the incessant coughing. I noticed that it seemed to get worse during the night. In the summer when my windows were open I could hear patients coughing all the way from another ward. It never seemed to stop.

As soon as their diagnostic tests showed improvement patients were transferred to the semi-ambulatory wards. Men went to E-2 and women to D-2. Here they began the second stage of their cure. It was called self-care. They were now granted privileges, one at a time. The first one allowed them to use the bathrooms, and the next one gave them permission to shower. After that the next step was being able to have their meals in the floor dining room. If they could tolerate this level of activity, and if their diagnostic tests remained the same, they were transferred to the E-1 and D-1 ambulatory wards to begin the final stages of their cure. Unless they suffered a relapse they were on their way to being discharged.

Everyone on these wards was also carefully monitored and continued to receive privileges. These were granted one at a time, unless symptoms or diagnostic tests showed evidence of relapse. For the first time since admission they could now wear their regular clothes. All meals were then taken in the main dining room. An additional perk that they had was that they were now allowed to visit patients on other wards.

Patients with full privileges could even have part-time jobs. Some helped out in the post office, store, library or greenhouse. These jobs were an important part in preparing people for discharge and for future employment. Those with teaching degrees were encouraged to teach the children. These jobs did not pay anything, but they were an extremely important part in rehabilitation.

Once they were granted outdoor privileges for scheduled amounts of time a whole new world opened up to them. They were now able to walk everywhere on the campus and hike on the trails in the thick woods between the sanitarium and the lake. Picnic areas equipped with tables and fireplaces were located near a winding stream. Its waters ran along the woods as it wound its way down toward the lake. Picking strawberries in the summer was a favorite pastime. Croquet was very popular and teams were formed. It became very competitive and there was a great deal of excitement during the games. Some patients went outside to cheer their favorite team on, while others cheered from their windows.

It is no wonder that Biggs was often referred to as a country club. If one were driving by and did not know this was a sanitarium it would be easy to assume that it was a summer resort. It also came as no surprise that many patients actually did not want to leave and dreaded being discharged. They became used to institutional life, and at Biggs once you were ambulatory life was quite pleasant — especially if you were single, or pretended that you were.

When people were cured there was much excitement. They were leaving the comfort of Biggs, they were cured, and they were returning home. Unfortunately the paradox was that the state spent a huge amount of money in curing patients who then were returned to the same environment that put them there in the first place. Once discharged they still had to be monitored through medical checkups and periodic chest x-rays. Again they had to make mental and physical adjustments. Those who wanted to return to work had to find employment that did not require a lot of physical strength. For many that meant changing their occupations. Sometimes employers refused them jobs even though their disease was arrested. Many people decided to complete or further their education.

Road to Recovery

After I had been hospitalized for seven years, my x-rays continued to show very little improvement in bone formation. My hip still retained only one-third of its normal motion. There was very little evidence of the remaining portion of the neck and no evidence of the head to the femur. Five to seven pounds of traction were applied for two months before another cast was applied. For more than a year the same treatment prevailed and there was no improvement. There continued to be definite progression of the disease, and by then there was atrophy (deterioration) of the femur. This included complete destruction of the head and neck.

By now my parents were starting to give up hope that I would ever be well enough to return home. They were told again and again that because of x-ray findings it would not be in my best interest to undergo surgery. Only continued supportive treatment was in order. Doctors still had hope that with the passage of time a fusion of the joint would occur so that weight could be borne. Even the localized cold abscesses were non-operable because of my condition. My parents became more and more frustrated with the words "with the passage of time."

Just before my twelfth birthday progress was shown in my condition. This news was the best birthday present ever. My hip showed free motion in almost all directions, although there was limitation in flexion. X-rays suggested no change. It was believed that at last the disease was finally conquered with "the passage of time." Millions of squadrons of microscopic bacilli had apparently surrendered. My favorite x-ray technician was a young man who for many years had always tried to put me at ease during the long hours I spent on the hard table waiting for the films to be read. He loved to tell jokes and reminded me of Peter, the orderly who had been so much fun years ago. Once I had received this good news he insisted that he was the one who had seen the tiny white flags of surrender on my x-rays. Naïve as I was at the time, I actually believed him!

After one more spica cast was applied, a decision had to be made on how my case would now be handled. A new program would have to be set up if conditions remained the same. However it was not until more than a year later that the cast was partially removed. It was cut down just a little at a time, a process that went on for several weeks. My skin felt wonderful as more and more areas of my body were uncovered. Now it was a daily ritual to have my skin washed with warm water and dried with a soft towel. It had been such a long time since I could touch the parts of my body that had been covered. How I loved to touch my skin, to rub it, just to feel it. Often when I had the full spica and felt an itch I could not reach I was so uncomfortable. My only solution was to use a knitting needle and try to locate the area bothering me. I am sure I drew blood on many occasions.

My hip had undergone a massive disease process for more than eight years. What a shock it was to me to now discover that my left leg was so much shorter and smaller than my right one. My left knee joint was very unsteady. According to my chart, my knee had "an abnormal degree of lateral mobility while in extension." Now it was necessary for this leg that had been kept immobile for so long to be exercised daily, and for my unstable knee to be massaged and stretched just within the limits of pain. Sometimes I would cry out because it hurt so much. Then the therapist would stop and go back to working on areas that were not as painful. As a result of this therapy my range of motion and flexion improved. I am sure it was worth all of the pain, although I did not think so at the time.

Once my cast was removed my doctors noticed an abnormal curvature of my spine called scoliosis. It resulted in considerable deformity of my chest with diminished breath sounds. My doctors believed these conditions were due to poor posture resulting from the deformity of my leg. They were unable to do anything about it but were confident that this condition would improve once I started walking—"in the passage of time."

While most young girls entering their teens were thinking about boys, going to parties and dances, and attending school functions and all of the other social activities that took place at that age, my thoughts were different.

Would this take another eight years?

Would there be more setbacks?

Would my life ever be normal?

Instead of rejoicing with the news of my progress I became very depressed, weeping into my pillow at night. Not much was known about depression in children then. Everyone thought I was just feeling a little sad. Several weeks went by and then one day a nurse appeared with my first pair of crutches. Now I had something to look forward to. This would be the first step in my being able to walk, and I slowly began to feel better.

While making their monthly rounds the orthopedic doctors started talking about the possibility of my having surgery. Their final decision, however, was that it was too much of a risk. There was too much destruction of bone, and there was the possibility of the bovine bacilli appearing again, or even perhaps settling in another bony area. Often I wondered if these tiny germs would ever leave my body — if my nightly prayers for recovery would ever be answered. My knee remained unstable, but the muscles of my left lower leg gained strength. Soon there was no evidence of the diminished breath sounds or scoliosis.

Walking on crutches was very difficult. I was so excited at the prospect of actually standing up, but when the staff tried to get me in a standing position I often felt dizzy. They would have to stop for a while and then try again and again. My greatest fear was of falling and so I took very small steps at first. After practicing for a while it was such a relief to get back into the wheelchair. Where before I had whizzed around at great speeds, now I was going at an extremely slow pace. It took several weeks, but every day I walked a little faster and went a little longer distance. My fellow patients on the ward cheered me on as I passed their rooms. It was a great thrill the day I finally walked the entire one-eighth of a mile, the length of the ward. Although I was very tired, I knew that if I could manage this distance I would continue to be able to handle walking further and further each day. Soon I became comfortable using crutches, but I looked forward to the day when I would be able to wear a shoe on both feet instead of just the right one.

Being on crutches did have certain advantages. For one thing, I now had unlimited outdoor exercise. The first place I headed for on my crutches was outdoors. There were so many places I could now explore — places that I had been unable to go in a wheelchair.

Now I could walk on the winding cinder paths and explore the wooded area on the hills between the main campus and the lake below. When I first saw the creek with its sparkling clear water and layers of different sizes and shapes of rocks, I was surprised by how lovely it was. I'd heard so much about it, but it was not the same as actually being there. I listened to the water cascade as it traveled down towards the lake and watched the tiny ripples and waves it created.

Once I found a large flat rock in the stream and discovered that I could very easily sit down on it, carefully placing my crutches at my side. Then I got braver and, with the help of my crutches, started wading into the deeper water. I was careful not to slip on the stones and pebbles. When I sat on this rock I could dangle my feet in the cool refreshing water. Of course the staff would have been furious if they knew what I was doing, but they never found out. There were so many things that I had done over the years that they never found out — things that were my own private adventures.

There were lifelike concrete statues of wildlife along the trail. They resembled the ones that were at the entrance of the children's building at Homer Folks. Perhaps these silent creatures stood guard on the grounds of all of the state sanitariums.

In this quiet haven the only sounds were those of birds and small animals. This became the place where I spent hours daydreaming about everything I wanted to do once I was discharged. I wanted to go to a real school, to take piano and swimming lessons, and to ride a bike. Perhaps I would take flying lessons and have my own plane. Then I would soar above the ground. This time I would actually fly.

Couples holding hands often walked in this private wooded area. When I took my walks alone on the trails I often found couples embracing and kissing, and I had heard rumors that they often went off the trails and into the tall grass where they had more privacy. With spouses and friends left behind, patients often found their intimacy within their own closed community.

Patients who were now separated from their homes, families and friends found that they had a lot of time on their hands. They did not have the responsibilities of running a household, raising children, or going to work. Concentration on getting well and waiting for the periodic testing placed the greatest stress on them. Those that had been here for months and even years were usually over their initial unhappiness, frustration, and depression. It must have been even harder for those who were married and who had children to cope with living in this closed structured environment. Perhaps for these reasons, combined with the average age of the patients, it was not unusual for romantic relationships to take place.

There has been some research on the behavior of tubercular patients in sanitariums. All kinds of surveys have been published. There have been conflicting reports about whether or not the sexual urge of these patients increased or decreased once they were institutionalized. As a young girl not yet in my teens I did not know anything about sexual urges. Years later as I thought about it, I realized that at Biggs these urges certainly appeared to have been increased.

In sanitariums across the country romantic relationships between patients was called cousining. Staff members worried about these liaisons because of their concern that a pregnancy would result. Many sanitariums had all kinds of rules and regulations that made it difficult for patients to cousin, but at Biggs the staff appeared to just look the other way. Often I heard sexual innuendoes that I did not understand.

There was constant gossip about which couples were going steady or had ended their relationships. Our male patient reporters were ruthless in reporting these affairs, as well as the times they discovered that one of the men had climbed into the window of a female patient. Of course these visits were prearranged, and windows were left unlocked on the night of the encounter. Patients loved reading about these humorous reports.

> John Smith sure enjoys visiting the ladies. We understand that his nocturnal visits are well received. To date he still has not been caught, although we understand that one night he had to hide under a certain young lady's bed when one of the night nurses was sure she had heard some very strange noises.

They also seemed to take great pleasure in reporting the names of the men who visited the wards of the new admissions. Every time a new female was admitted to C-1 one of the roving reporters carefully checked her out and then reported back to the others. With luck (for the men) these women would be on an ambulatory ward within a few months and would then be available for dating. One extremely popular young man was called gorgeous George, and another earned the reputation of being a lover boy. He was called Romeo. There was constant flirting with the student nurses, and they seemed to enjoy it as much as the in-house Romeos.

Although it was also frowned on by the administration, there were often situations in which a relationship developed between a patient and a staff member. There were a number of couples that became engaged while I was there and later we would hear about them getting married after discharge. One of these was Anna, a freelance artist who gave me lessons in painting. She became engaged to a young man who worked in maintenance. He visited her every day. We all went down to her room to congratulate her and admire her engagement ring. They were married soon after she was discharged.

Beginning with Peter, the adventurous young orderly, there were several friends that I developed a crush on. Once I left H building I never saw Peter again, but I never forgot him and the wonderful friendship we had. Then there had been Warren, the boy who had flown his kite and demonstrated his biking skills on the lawn beneath my second story window at H. When he told me his family was moving, and as we said good-bye, he had leaned over and kissed me gently on my lips. It was sweet, it was innocent, and it was my first kiss. When I discovered the magnificent voice of young Frank Sinatra on my radio I developed a crush on him that lasted for years. In my fantasies he drove to the hospital, placed me in a luxurious convertible, and drove me to Hollywood. There we were married and lived the proverbial happily ever after.

A crush on an older man on the men's ward — he must have been all of twenty — led to my actually stalking him. Of course I did not know what stalking was — let us just say I made it a point whenever possible to just happen to be wherever he was. He was an extremely handsome Italian American and looked something like my young uncles. With his tightly curled black hair and big brown eyes he was even better looking than my Frankie, although he could not sing at all. He was often teased when he joined the group singing around the piano in the day room, although the girls didn't seem to mind his being tone deaf. Even my friend Carol, along with most of the young women on the ward, was in love with him. They were more subtle about it than I was. He was nicknamed Liberty when our roving reporters took note of the fact that he often took liberties with his adoring fans.

When I thought he would not notice, I followed him around everywhere. I tried to sit as close to him as I could whenever he was in the auditorium, dining room or day room. Sometimes he talked to me. I tried to remember every single word he said so that I could tell my roommate about it.

One day I was looking out of my window and I saw him coming from the trails with his arms around a young woman who had recently been admitted to my ward. From a distance it looked like Carol. They stopped, embraced and kissed. My heart was broken, although I was relieved the women was not my friend. From that day on I stopped stalking him. So much for older men. They just were not worth the trouble.

* * *

Now that I was able to use crutches my parents obtained permission to take me on short excursions away from the hospital. There are many beautiful parks in Ithaca, but it was Stewart Park that was our favorite. This lakeside municipal park was level and easier to get around in. There was a duck pond and bird sanctuary that I never got tired of seeing. Although I begged my father to carry me onto one of the park's rowboats, he did not think it would be safe. Later he told me that as a child he had almost drowned, that he had never learned to swim. He still had a fear of the water.

Two state parks that we also enjoyed were Taughanock and Buttermilk Falls. Taughanock Falls are smaller than Niagara Falls, but they are actually higher. They are breathtaking as they plunge through a huge rock amphitheater. Buttermilk Falls descends into cascades and rapids, forming a natural pool at the bottom that is used by swimmers. This was the first time in my life I had seen people swim. How I envied them.

It is no wonder that the movie industry once flourished in Ithaca. The natural beauty of the area, with its scenic rugged gorges, glens and falls was perfect for background scenes in many Hollywood movies.

Now that I was allowed to leave the sanitarium so often, and for longer and longer lengths of time, my parents began to talk about the possibility of bringing me home. They were beginning to feel that there was nothing that was being done for me at Biggs that they could not do for me at home. We were picnicking at one of the parks and for the first time in a long time my parents did not seem quite as tense as they discussed this. My father had pointed out that he had noticed that all of those patients who have tuberculosis of the lung go home once they have reached the end of their cure. My parents' only problem at the time was knowing whether or not the doctors thought that I had reached the end of mine. After that they talked about it to each other frequently when they came to visit, but did not ask my doctors if I could be discharged. They still had absolute faith in them and did not like to question them.

My father was right in his observation of discharges of pulmonary patients who were cured. We were all so excited when someone had reached this stage and was able to return home. Yet, since pulmonary tuberculosis was potentially a recurring disease, there was always the fear of being readmitted, of having to start all over again once they were admitted to the ambulatory ward. It was not uncommon to hear that someone we knew had been readmitted after being discharged. This had to be even more upsetting than the original admission. Those of us with bone tuberculosis seldom had this problem, but there was always the fear of contracting the pulmonary disease.

*   *   *

In July of 1945, after nine years, I was finally discharged. According to my medical records, I had received maximum hospital benefit. My parents, who had grown weary of my constant hospitalization, finally had discussed this with the medical staff. When the doctors got together to discuss it, they were not all in agreement that it was time for me to return home. When they finally gave in and gave their consent they made my parents promise that they would bring me back as an outpatient for constant observation until I was officially cured. It was documented in my chart that my "prognosis for a long life expectancy was good, but for recovery from the disease was poor."

Needless to say there was a great deal of excitement when word got out that I was going home. Everyone made such a fuss over it, and I got caught up with their words of encouragement and support. My friends were happy for me and told me how much they would miss me, and I knew I would miss this family as well. A great send-off, complete with brightly colored balloons and flowers, was held in my honor on the day before I left.

Elena seemed to be the one most upset by my leaving. Just before the day I left she told me how much she would miss me, and that it just wouldn't be the same without me. She wondered if she would ever see me again. We hugged, and I told her not to worry and that my parents had promised to bring me back to visit everyone — and especially her. It was hard to say goodbye to those people I was the closest to, especially Elena, Carol, and my roommate Jean.

When I started packing my belongings into the suitcases and boxes my parents had left on their last visit I asked Jean if she would like to have some of my books and games. She was delighted to have them and I brought them over and placed them on her nightstand. Jean made me promise that I would write and tell her everything once I got home, and that I would behave myself in school. My quiet roommate had finally begun to acquire a sense of humor.

On the morning of my long-awaited discharge I could not eat my breakfast. I was too excited. When my parents arrived to get me they were the happiest I had ever seen them. My father was singing as he put my belongings into the car. As we drove towards the entrance my father stopped the car to turn onto the main highway. When I looked back at the grounds and buildings of what had been home to me for the last five years I began to feel anxious. I had no idea what was going to happen next or what living at home would be like. At Biggs I had somehow been happy and I wanted to stay that way. There had always been so many things to do, and I was not sure there would be at home. My friends were always there in the sanitarium, but I did not know if I would have friends at home, or what a real school would be like. It would not be long before I would find the answers to my questions and concerns.

Home At Last

No one had prepared me in any way for this very difficult transition to living at home. My discharge plan had addressed only the dates of my outpatient appointments, as well as follow-up supervision by the public health department in the county I lived in.

Prior to my discharge my parents lived in a small apartment. It was not large enough for a family of four. Other arrangements had to be made before I could come home. They had no money to purchase a house and were unable to find a downstairs apartment. Once again our family came to our aid. We were invited to live with my mother's elderly aunt and uncle, Margaret and Peter Pravi. Their small house, located in an older neighborhood of Seneca Falls, became our home.

This great aunt and uncle were friendly enough, but it was impossible for me to communicate with them. They had immigrated here about the same time as my grandparents and spoke only in their native language. Perhaps since they did not have children they did not feel a need to learn the new language. My parents spoke fluent Italian. Maryann, who now was four years old, was able to understand the Italian spoken because she was constantly exposed to it. She even spoke a few words of it herself. It really frustrated me and made me feel even more left out than I already did. No one offered to teach me this beautiful-sounding language, and I never asked. It sounded a lot like the few words in Spanish I had learned while at Biggs. Once I began to recognize some of the language it was easier. Still it was not until much later in my life that I realized that it would have been the perfect opportunity to learn to speak Italian. Instead I was often impatient at having to

After nine consecutive years of hospitalization I am home at last in 1944.

listen to it, and I was constantly interrupting to ask, "What did you say?" Italians talk with their hands a lot — a sort of sign language. Many, particularly the men, used various hand gestures. When I asked my great-uncle what one of them meant when two of my uncles were arguing, he just smiled and shook his head, muttering something to himself in Italian.

With the exception of what I had learned while talking to my grandparents at Biggs, I had not grasped the fact that I was an Italian American. Now that I was living at home I realized that it was not just the language that my relatives and their friends continued to speak. They carried on the traditions and customs of their homeland, but as time went on the younger generations often did not carry them on. The kitchen was always the main gathering place of the home while the living room was rarely used. Meals were divided into four parts and had a definite pattern. They started with some kind of pasta, then an entrée, then salad with vegetables, and ended with dessert. It was difficult for me to become accustomed to this food after eating the food in the hospital. There was not the variety I was used to and I found the food too spicy.

All of the rooms in this house were so small and I felt claustrophobic, closed in. Sometimes I felt like I could not breathe. There was no privacy unless I went into my tiny bedroom. My mother had made a beautiful spread for my bed, but the mattress was so soft I could not get used to it. There was not enough storage space to hold my belongings. At least this room was mine, and it soon became my retreat. When I felt depressed, which was most of the time, I just went to my room and closed the door. My body would shake and I would go into a cold sweat. Sometimes I would start to cry, so I put my head under my pillow to muffle the sound.

Perhaps it would have helped if I had things to do. All of the activities I had enjoyed at Biggs were no longer available to me. My mother refused to let me help with any housework. No one had me help in preparing meals or taught me how to cook or bake. While everyone else was busy I felt useless and unwanted. Again I disappeared into a world of books and dreams. When I looked out of my bedroom window or sat on the small front porch I saw children going by. Some were on bikes, others were running and shouting to one another. They were indeed the happy children, while I remained one of the lost.

Everything in my life was now so different. The organized schedules and routines that I had grown up with were now a thing of the past. Even the food was different. It tasted very good, but there was not the variety of meals that I was used to. In the kitchen there was a constant pleasant aroma of tomato sauce — my family called it gravy. I loved the smell of their freshly brewed coffee, fresh basil and other herbs, and even the sautéed garlic. It was all new to me. Later I learned that practically every Italian American family served pasta with meatballs and other types of meat, a garden salad prepared with olive oil and vinegar, and fresh Italian bread. every Sunday for dinner. Almost without exception this meal took place around noon, usually after church. Nearly every one of my relatives who had a house had a small vegetable and herb garden in their yard.

One thing that I found especially upsetting in this new environment was discovering that my parents were constantly arguing. There had been times at Biggs when they were obviously unhappy and not getting along, but it was nothing like this. Now I was seeing something very troubling. There were days when they did not speak to each other. Because I was so centered on my own unhappiness, I failed to realize that this move, along with the new responsibility of taking care of a handicapped child, was something they were having difficulty dealing with. Their very limited income had to be a major concern as well. Sometimes I wondered if it was something I said or did, or perhaps they really didn't want me there. Our relatives who had taken us in were no help at all. It was a stressful time for all of us. Maryann was the only one who seemed happy, although I sometimes wonder if it had an effect on her that I was not aware of.

There was a steady stream of friends and relatives who came to welcome me home. They were not at all like the people that I had known. It seemed that they talked and laughed very loudly. Sometimes they argued with one another. They talked about things that I knew nothing about: people they knew, and what was going on in town and in the neighborhood. Often they spoke a mixture of English and Italian. Everyone talked about money and jobs. These were things I had never given any thought to. For the first time in my life I began to realize that people had different incomes and standards of living, and that my parents were very poor. Ironically, everyone in the institutions I was in thought I was very rich because of all the things that were constantly being given to me. Finding out that I was a member of a poor family was upsetting to me.

Our relatives were constantly celebrating some special occasion — birthdays, holidays and festivals. Weddings took place over several days and usually everyone in the family was involved in some way. My mother often made the wedding and bridesmaids' dresses. As Catholics they also celebrated each child's baptism, communion and confirmation. In between these events there was constant visiting back and forth among the families. No one ever bothered to call ahead but was always welcomed when they appeared at the door. It was the custom to put on a pot of coffee and offer food as soon as they arrived.

All of this activity cheered me up somewhat, but I longed to be with children my own age. How I missed my family at Biggs. Here I did not have a single friend. I did not like this tiny house or this new life. It was exhausting. All I could think of was that perhaps things would get better when school started.

It seemed as though people used their cars constantly, even when they went short distances. Although I had ridden in a car, riding on a bus or train was completely new to me. Shopping downtown in our small village was also a new experience. There were all of these little shops and places to eat. Until then I had never been in a restaurant or had an ice cream sundae. My only shopping experience had been the tiny store on Main Street at Biggs. When my mother took me into the city of Syracuse to shop for school clothes I was amazed at the size of the large department stores and the large selection of merchandise that was available. There were so many choices.

My father was now employed as a core maker in a nearby factory, where he worked the second shift. Since he would leave in the afternoon and not get home until after I went to bed, I did not see him that much. Mom continued to make and alter clothes for her growing number of customers. Still their combined income was not enough to support our family. Up until now the state of New York had completely paid for my care. Traveling to see me was the only expense my family had in my long hospitalization.

My mom's sister Mary and her husband Jerry bought the house next door to us. They were my godparents and had been frequent visitors during my long confinement. Now I would be able to see them every day. Their house had an interesting history which was depicted by a small sign in the front yard. It had been the home of Elizabeth Cady Stanton, one of the leaders in the movement for women's suffrage in the 1800s. It wasn't until I was in school that I learned more about this historic movement, and how it led to the first Women's Rights Convention held in Seneca Falls in 1848. My relatives seemed to have no knowledge of Elizabeth Cady Stanton or the significance of the sign. Their interest was in the history of Italy and they did not embrace that of this country. No one in my family had a high school education, and in fact many had only completed a few years of elementary school. Although they knew little about American history, they had a great deal of knowledge about their homeland, culture and religion. My grandparents read the Italian newspaper and were well informed about current events in Italy. Grandma Adele still thought that Mussolini was a great man, and no one could convince her otherwise. Eventually the Stanton House was purchased and restored by the federal government. It is now a major tourist attraction. Years later the government purchased the little house that we had lived in and had it torn down in order to expand the grounds of the Stanton House.

It soon became apparent that six people could not live in such cramped quarters. Even if that was not the case, my parents began to realize that this house was too far for me to walk to Mynderse Academy, the public school I would be attending. Climbing into and riding a bus would not have been easy for me. Although I was walking without a cane or crutches, I walked slower than normal and tired easily.

With the help of my mother's family my parents purchased a house about a block from the school. It needed a lot of work. My grandfather and several of his sons donated their expert carpentry skills and remodeled the house to fit our needs. They replaced the steep staircase with one that had a landing and was easier for me to climb. My favorite part of this house was the front porch. Unlike the quiet neighborhood we had moved from, this was a very busy street. Neighbors stopped by to visit us on the porch.

It was very important to my mother that I be well dressed for school. In addition to the clothes we got in the city, she made several beautiful dresses and skirts for me. She loved clothes and fashion and was always talking about the latest styles. These things were not important to me. My needs were different. I was nervous about attending school, and had still not gotten used to living at home.

On the morning of my first day of school my mother made a special breakfast, but I was too keyed up to eat. When I put on a new dress that my mother picked out from my school wardrobe my father looked at me and smiled. He put his arms around me and told me how beautiful I looked. He offered to walk the short distance to the school with me, but I refused. This was something I had to do on my own. As I walked cautiously to the entrance of the school students passed me in a rush to find their homerooms. There was a great deal of shouting and laughter as they greeted one another. No one seemed to notice me. When I entered my homeroom everyone else was already seated. Our teacher was getting everyone to settle down. When she saw me she introduced me to the class and told me which desk was mine. As I walked slowly to my desk, being careful not to fall on the slippery waxed floor, my classmates stared at me curiously. How I wanted to walk away, to avoid their curious stares, and to return to the safety of my home. I felt so self-conscious and for the first time in my life, realizing how different I was, felt ashamed and embarrassed.

During my long hospital stay I never felt different than other children. Despite my long illness and frequent episodes of depression, I had become used to institutional life. It was really all I knew. It was safe. In many ways I felt luckier than so many patients I knew who were less fortunate than I. Once I was in a wheelchair I enjoyed the freedom to explore the buildings and grounds and was actively involved in many activities. My parents visited every Sunday, and I absolutely loved my extended hospital family. Now that part of my life was over.

Those first few days were the hardest, although I soon discovered how kind my classmates were. They tried to help me by offering to carry my books, or taking my arm when I had to climb the stairs to get to a class. A part of me really appreciated these gestures, but still I often resented their offers of help because I did not want to be dependent on them.

It was difficult to make friends, and much of that was my own fault. I became quiet, intimidated by all that was going on around me. Other children talked about and were involved in so many things I knew nothing about. In many ways I seemed more mature than they were, but socially it was another story. At Biggs I had become very outgoing and sociable — a leader of the other children and included in many activities with the adults. Now I was suddenly shy, barely spoke to anyone, and once again retreated into my own private world.

* * *

Mynderse Academy was named after Wilhelmus Mynderse, an entrepreneur who more than any other individual was responsible for the growth and prosperity of Seneca Falls. Previously it had been a private school, but now was part of the public school system. Grades seven through twelve were located there.

There were no records of what grades I had completed. Since I was thirteen years old, school officials decided to place me in the eighth grade. Classes were divided into three groups — A, B, and C. Those students who were the brightest were placed in group A. Since there were no records of my previous grades I was enrolled in group C. This group proved much too easy for me. After the first marking period I was placed in the more challenging group A.

Although I had not taken many of the courses mandated by the public schools, my experiences at Biggs had in many ways been an advantage to me scholastically. Extensive reading had made up for many of the courses I had missed. Living in an environment which consisted mainly of adults had been a learning experience in itself.

Early and constant exposure to the fine arts had enriched my life. At home I would never have had this advantage. My participation in writing for the hospital newspaper, helping out at the radio station, and tutoring younger children were just a few of the wide range of things I had done. Projects in occupational therapy had also been an excellent outlet, offering me a chance to be creative in so many ways.

One of the reasons it was hard to make friends was because everyone seemed to be in one little clique or another. This was especially true of the girls. As I watched and listened to them I categorized them into four separate groups. First came what I called sorority sisters. These were the most popular girls. They were all very attractive and socially active. If you were lucky you got invited to one of their slumber parties. Many of them were cheerleaders and the darlings of the boys' athletic teams. At formal dances such as the prom it seemed they were always on the court, either as one of the princesses or even as a queen. Next were the groups I called friends. This was a mixed group that included both girls who had transferred from the local Catholic school, Saint Patrick's, or who had grown up together and usually lived in the same neighborhood. These friends stayed together and were the friendliest group, the one that was more likely to befriend new students.

Sometimes your group was defined by your activity. There were a few who today would have been called geeks. They were the top students, who were consistently on the honor roll, held offices in various clubs, and were leaders in student government. It was not uncommon to cross over from one group to another.

Loners were the name I gave the fourth group. This group consisted mainly of students who did not live in town and rode buses to and from the school. They did not get together very often with those who lived in the village because the buses left right after dismissal. This also meant that they missed out on a lot of after-school activities. While the students called walkers went downtown for Cokes or took part in after-school activities, those who lived in rural areas went home. On the weekend they rarely came back into town to attend sporting events or go to the Barn, a recreation center where teenagers got together to mingle and dance. Other loners included students who seemed to have no friends, kept to themselves, and rarely participated in school activities.

For the first few months I kept to myself and was a very unhappy loner. After a while I started making friends with girls in the friends group, and soon I found myself included. As time went on I became so engrossed in my studies and school activities that I occasionally crossed over to the geeks, holding an office in student government and remaining on the high honor roll right up to graduation. I never did become a sorority sister. Disabled students were never cheerleaders, and I could only dream about being a princess or even a queen.

*   *   *

It was difficult to try to fit in, be like everyone else, when so many accommodations were made for me. Before 1990 when the Americans with Disabilities Act (ADA) was passed, it was up to the individual schools to decide what could be done for students with disabilities. In my case the administration felt that it would not be safe for me to use the regular stairs where students rushed up and down to get to classes between bells. There was a fear that I would trip or fall. As a safety measure this problem was resolved by allowing me to use the open marble staircase inside the school's main entrance. Only members of the staff and seniors were allowed to use these stairs. It was the school's way of doing something special for the graduating class, and the stairs were referred to as the "senior stairs."

Physical education was a required class but I was exempt from it. Instead I spent that time alone in my homeroom. If the door to the downstairs gym was open I could hear the gym teacher's whistle and the shouts of my classmates. It was hard to sit there while they seemed to be having such a good time. Girls in my class had an even better time when the woman who taught science and was the girl's physical education teacher had to leave. She was replaced by a nice-looking young man who soon became very popular with all of the students. It was the first time a man had been in charge of the girls' gym class and many of his adoring students had a crush on him. Our senior class dedicated our yearbook to him. He was invited to all of our class reunions, and over the years missed very few.

Mynderse did not have a cafeteria and, with the exception of the bus students, everyone was allowed to go home for lunch. Although I lived only one block away, I was told that I could eat my lunch in my homeroom. Occasionally a bus student joined me, but usually I sat alone and ate the lunch that my mother had prepared and placed in a brown paper bag.

Once a week there was an early dismissal for students to attend religious education at whatever church they belonged to. Catholic students walked to Saint Patrick's Church. This church was quite a long distance from the school and so I was not able to attend. My parents were unable to drive me there as my father was still working a second shift and my mother did not have her driver's license yet.

Not being able to take religious education turned out to be a problem the year I was to be confirmed. Confirmation is a rite which acknowledges that the candidate is now able to fully participate in the church. There were several required classes and rehearsals in the church prior to this event and everyone had to attend them — everyone but me. All of the children in the confirmation class were much younger than I. My classmates who were Catholic had been confirmed earlier. How out of place I felt with these younger children.

During the final rehearsal I was allowed to join the procession as the children walked down the aisle to the altar. As I proudly walked with the class I soon found that I could not keep up with them so I returned to my seat and watched. On the day of confirmation I wore a lovely white dress that my mother made for me. It was decided that I would walk in back of the class. At the last moment one of the nuns approached me and said they had changed their minds and escorted me to a room in back of the altar. There I sat alone and waited to be confirmed. No one saw my beautiful dress. No one saw my tears.

*   *   *

Just a few months after entering school I had a very upsetting outpatient appointment. Dr. Severson, who had taken care of me for years at Biggs, told me I had to have surgery on my right leg in order to prevent it from growing any longer. My parents were as upset as I was and wanted more information about it. He explained that in order to prevent the increasingly rapid growth of my right leg something had to be done to stop it. This surgery was called an epiphyseal arrest. Bone growth takes place in the growth plates (physes), the area of growing tissue found near the end of the long bones in children and adolescents. Each long bone has at least two growth plates that determine the future length and shape of the mature bone. If I did not have this surgery the difference in the length of my legs would become so great that walking would be impossible. They had estimated by the height of my parents that I had almost reached my projected adult height. Dr. Severson recommended that this surgery take place as soon as possible.

Surgery was immediately scheduled at Syracuse University Hospital for just after Christmas. This would give me time to recuperate during the holiday and not miss too much school. All of the orthopedic surgeons who traveled to Biggs to care for patients with bone tuberculosis, including Dr. Severson, had practices there. He tried to set my mind at ease about this unexpected hospitalization. It was very hard for me to accept the fact that they were going to perform an operation on my right leg — the good leg. It was also very hard for me to accept the fact that my first Christmas after returning home would be overshadowed by having this surgery.

My surgery went well and this time the cast that was applied just covered my right leg. There was not much pain following this operation, and it was not necessary to keep me in the hospital more than a few weeks. My recollections of the details of being admitted to this hospital and operated on are not clear. It may have been because I did not ever want to think about it or talk about it to anyone once I was discharged. There was one exception, however. When I returned to the hospital for a follow-up several weeks later Dr. Severson removed the stitches from my leg. There were six incisions in all, one on each side of my ankle and four around my knee. My mother was at my side when the stitches were removed. She became so upset when she saw the ugly jagged surgical scars covered with dried blood that she passed out and had to be revived.

When I returned home I discovered that my bed had been moved downstairs into the living room. Once again I had to start using first crutches and then a cane. This time I accomplished this in a very short period of time. Even though part of my recovery time took place during the holiday break, I was unable to attend school for several additional weeks.

Once I was comfortable using crutches the next step was to be fitted for shoes.

*   *   *

Since my left foot was so much smaller than my right I needed two different sizes. For the rest of my life whenever I would purchase new shoes two of them had to be discarded. It took my parents a long time to find a cobbler who would attempt to make and attach a five-inch lift to my smaller shoe. When they found one who agreed to tackle this job he explained that it would be very expensive. First he would have to remove the sole of the shoe and then carve a lift out of wood. Next he had to attach the lift, replace the sole, and then glue on a piece of leather to match the shoe. It would cost several hundred dollars by the time the shoes were finished.

On the day that I saw the completed work I was horrified. The orthopedic shoe with the lift was dreadful looking and I did not even want to try it on. It looked so huge. Both shoes were black and had shoelaces. When the cobbler, noticing my tears, tried to cheer me up by telling me that these shoes often came in dark brown as well, it did not help. At that time shoes like these were often referred to as granny shoes, but even my two grandmothers wore shoes more fashionable than mine.

"I will never wear those ugly things," I remember saying angrily, "they look terrible." Of course I had no choice if I were to walk without crutches. Since the left shoe was so heavy, and the lift was not shaped to provide proper balance, walking was difficult. If I was not careful I would fall. Stepping on something as tiny as a pebble would throw me off balance. All of the problems I faced were not the fault of the cobbler. When I stood upright my hips were tilted because the lift, although quite high, was not high enough. This put a great deal of pressure on my spine, a condition that would always give me problems. Still, the doctors continued to explain as they monitored my progress, if the lift were any higher it would have been impossible for me to walk at all.

Walking slower than normal with an unsteady gait continued to be a problem, and I always tired easily when I had to walk a long distance. Frustrated with my constant struggle and unsteady walking, my parents started searching for a different cobbler. Over the years they tried many different ones. These men, just like the first one who had taken care of us, were always older men who had emigrated from Italy. Since they spoke very little English they were pleasantly surprised when my mother spoke to them in Italian. They all had years of experience in the shoe-making skills that their ancestors had developed over centuries. Although they were excellent craftsmen in making and repairing shoes, the lifts they put on my shoes were never just right.

One day my mother and I found a cobbler whose shop was located in the basement of a large department store. This man, who told us to call him Joe, told us that he had a daughter who was about the same age as me. As a result of polio she also wore a lift similar in size to mine. He had spent years perfecting a lift for her that was made of a lighter material and shaped in a way that made walking safer. When I told him I was so tired of the ugly shoes I had been wearing for years he told me that, due to popular demand, orthopedic shoes were now being made to look more stylish. They were now available in many different colors and textures, and sometimes had decorative accents as well. Unlike previous corrective shoes these were made to look more like non-orthopedic shoes. They were still made for balance and comfort. This was such great news for me and I was so excited that my mother let me order not one but two pairs. One pair I chose was a bright red and the other a soft white for summer. Gone were the days of the granny shoes. Instead of shoelaces these shoes had one or more straps on them. When Joe retired we had to find other cobblers. This time the results were better because they were able to work from existing shoes such as the ones Joe had made.

When I first starting walking on my own, and gradually as the years went by, I struggled with the limitations of my mobility. Little by little since I first entered college my ability to walk has consistently become more and more of a challenge. I have tried to remain as independent as possible as I went from using canes to crutches to finally a wheelchair or scooter.

Many years later I discovered a marvelous upscale shoe store. In addition to having a large variety of regular shoes, the store contained shoes for people with special needs for their feet. There they specialized in fitting, designing, making adjustments, and doing whatever else was needed in the shoes for people with genetic, diabetic, and foot and leg abnormalities. They were expert in the building and application of lifts such as mine for leg length discrepancies. On my first visit, with my orthopedic doctor's prescription in hand, I ordered my first pair. These shoes were so comfortable and made it much easier for me to stand and to walk.

One day I confided to the store's owner that when I was younger I would have given anything to wear high heels. We both laughed when he replied, "But Gloria, your lift would have had to be over a foot high." I am sure that sometimes the customers who overheard our conversations did not know what to make of them. It was fun to find some humor in a shoe store so different than the ones where I often left in tears. On another visit, after watching a customer walk around trying out a new chic pair of sneaks, I said that I had never even thought of wearing a pair of the ever-popular sneakers everyone seemed to have.

"It isn't that I did not want to," I explained, "but I was sure that it would be impossible to put a lift on them."

Again I was asked why I had never mentioned this before. I was told that many of the customers who shopped there wore sneakers with lifts. So that very day I was fitted for a pair of awesome white and silver sneakers. When I first wore them I realized why they were so popular. They were the most comfortable and lightweight shoes I had ever worn. When my grandsons saw them on me for the first time they thought that Nane was totally cool. Of course I draw the line at even suggesting that I buy a pair of the decorative flip flops that all of the cool people were wearing. Besides, having painted toenails would only increase people's curiosity about my lift.

So many stores now provide wheelchairs and scooters for shoppers who find walking difficult. A teenage girl approached me on a day when I was wearing my sneakers, zipping around a store in one of their scooters. Just for fun I had recently painted the Nike logo on my lift.

"Excuse me," she said, "where did you buy those great sneakers? I would really like to buy a pair just like them." Since she was standing on my left side she could only see the shoe with the lift.

Well, I thought, I could really have fun with this one. Instead I told her about the other sneaker. She was embarrassed, but then started to laugh when I told her I never dreamed that one day I could make a fashion statement for sneaker lovers everywhere.

After I started working and paying for my own health insurance I tried to get reimbursement for my shoes. Every insurance plan I had, regardless of accompanying letters from my doctors, turned me down. Orthopedic and corrective shoes were never covered. In my entire life I have seen only about half a dozen people with a lift as high as mine. Some people were managing on forearm crutches or using canes. Others walked with the same slow gait that I had. There were a few that I talked to, and they all said they had severe back problems and tired easily.

*　　*　　*

When I returned to school I had a lot of catching up to do. Although once again I tried to be more independent, there were things that I simply could not do. This was something I learned to accept. Teenage years are stressful for most young people. They are a time of discovery, a time of change. Your body is changing. You are no longer a child, yet you are still not an adult. Resentment towards authority often surfaces as teens become confused about their lives. For a disabled teenager these years can be especially difficult. You are considered different and you may be treated differently. More than ever you need to feel accepted by your peers. What you do not need is sympathy or, even worse, being left out of the gatherings and events enjoyed by other children.

It was lonesome walking the short block from my house to the school. Now that I was wearing my orthopedic shoes I was actually walking more slowly than I had been on my crutches. Boys and girls walked past me, hurrying along so they would not be late for school. One day a girl who had just moved into the neighborhood started walking with me. She introduced herself and told me she was in tenth grade. When she asked if she could walk to school with me every day I was overjoyed. About two weeks later I saw her walking on the other side of the street with some other girls. She put her head down when I looked over at her. When I ran into her a few days later and asked why she no longer walked with me she said it was making her late for class. She had not meant to upset me. Over the years as I gained strength my walking improved somewhat, but it was never normal. I got used to walking by myself, to people passing me by.

My classmates were never cruel to me as children often are to other children that are different. This is especially true in middle schools. In junior high I was never embarrassed or harassed by my classmates. They were very kind and, despite my constant struggle to be independent, eventually accepted me as one of them. They simply ignored my handicap, just as I tried to do.

*　　*　　*

In the 1920s through the 1940s American society as a whole was deeply prejudiced against the disabled. Author P. K. Longmore wrote, "They were kept at home, out of sight, in back bedrooms by families who felt a mixture of embarrassment and shame about their presence." In his book *FDR's Splendid Deception,* H. G. Gallagher wrote, "They were viewed as flawed in moral character as well as body." President Franklin Delano Roosevelt was stricken with polio at the age of thirty-nine. He was paralyzed from the waist down and never walked on his own again. He went to great lengths to conceal his disability from the public because he wanted everyone to see him as a strong leader. People never would elect him again if they saw him as a cripple. Was it to be the same with me? Did my friends see me as being crippled? I wanted my peers to see me as normal — as one of them. So I went on treating my disability as though it did not exist. Unlike the president, however, my disability could not be hidden. There were no secret service agents at my side guarding me or carrying me from room to room, vehicle to vehicle.

All of this had meant nothing to me at Biggs, but now that I was home I realized that people were constantly staring at me. First, after noticing my limp, they would look down at the lift on my shoe. Then they would look at me, usually with pity in their eyes. It was a source of constant irritation and somehow I just could not get over becoming embarrassed, humiliated and angry when this happened. Strangers often came right out and asked me what happened. Sometimes my answers were rude, especially when I was young. Other times I simply stared them down, causing them to be embarrassed as well. That made people uncomfortable and they usually just looked the other way. It was exactly what I wanted them to do. It was many years before I stopped getting upset by the intrusive questions and curious stares of insensitive and inquisitive people.

My mother was the only one that I confided in about my frustrations. Sometimes I took them out on her. She could not understand why I was often unhappy. After all I was home and in school. Her own life had not been an easy one, and compared to that she must have felt that I was just spoiled. Maybe she was right. Everyone had catered to me from the moment I first became sick. I found it was better to just keep my frustrations to myself and keep busy at home and in school.

Things started improving for us financially when my mother found a job as a seamstress in the New York Shop. This exclusive women's dress shop, located in nearby Auburn, sold very upscale clothing. She was put in charge of alterations and did such a good job that she brought in many customers. She traveled by bus every day, which meant that I had to help take care of Maryann when my father was also at work. Maryann and I were not only far apart in our ages, but in our interests as well. She was much more active and outgoing. Still we enjoyed one another, and as we got older the differences didn't seem to matter.

In school I actively participated in writing for the school paper as well as the yearbook. There were clubs for art, drama and library and I belonged to each of them. I was an officer in several organizations, including our student government.

My goal of learning to play the piano seemed impossible since we did not have one. How I missed the magnificent grand piano in the auditorium at Biggs. Even if my parents could have afforded one like that, it would have taken up our entire living room! They knew how much I wanted to take lessons and it wasn't long before a secondhand upright piano was delivered to our house. After taking lessons for a year I played in front of an audience twice. First it was during my piano teacher's recitals. I could not wait for it to be over as I was very nervous. Then in school when our class put on a variety show I had a piano solo. My selection, a popular song called "The Sunny Side of the Street," went over well. Again I found I could not wait until it was over, and after that I realized that I would never play in public again.

Speaking on stage in the auditorium or in front of the class did not have the same effect on me. In fact it was just the opposite. Public speaking excited me; it gave me a rush, and the more I spoke in public the more confident I became. Once shy in class, I now continually had my hand up to speak.

"Yes, Gloria," a young teacher once remarked when I raised my hand to answer a question, "but I think we should give someone else a chance to answer."

Even though I did not take physical education or play sports, I started attending the school's football and basketball games. When the games were held at other schools I went on our school's spectator bus, singing and shouting with my classmates. Sometimes I got a little carried away with the school songs and cheers, and before long I was writing some for the school. I loved writing lyrics that were humorous and fun to sing.

School was a constant challenge and I began to enjoy every minute of it, including homework and studying for tests. When an English teacher announced a five-hundred–word essay to be written you could hear the moans and groans of most of the class. Not me, I could not wait to begin the assignment. When a history teacher gave us a project that required that we draw and label maps, I could not wait to start on mine. There was never enough homework for me — I was definitely a geek.

Socially it was an entirely different story. Mynderse held many school dances throughout the year. Each class had its own annual dance, and sometimes after sporting events dances were held in the gymnasium. There were also often dances during the lunch hour. It seemed that dancing was an important part of those school years. There were also theme dances and — most exciting of all — the junior prom and senior ball. For weeks the decorating committee, which I always volunteered for, transformed the gymnasium into an amazing wonderland. Students selected a king, queen and court for these formal dances. It was frustrating to me not to be able to dance, and I never attended any of them. My only involvement in them was volunteering for the decorating and planning committees.

One day, shortly after a queen's court was announced, several of my friends confided in me that a number of students thought that I should have been nominated for princess. Although I was flattered by this, I realized how unrealistic it would have been. On the night that these dances took place I retreated into my imaginary world. There I danced the night away with whatever boy or movie star I had a crush on at the time hugging my pillow. I had outgrown Dopey.

On weekends most of my classmates gathered in the Barn, a small one-story building in back of one of the churches. For an admission fee of ten cents boys and girls got together to socialize and dance. A jukebox blared out the music of the forties. I did go there a few times, but found no pleasure in watching other people dance.

In the summer I took swimming lessons through the local chapter of the American Red Cross. Classes were held at Cayuga Lake State Park, just a few miles from my home. It was not long before I was swimming in deep water and jumping off a large raft. What a sense of freedom and independence being in the water gave me. It seemed I had found my sport. During the summer my father would drive my friends and me down to the park. We spent the entire day there. It was the place where everyone gathered, enjoying the pleasures of their summer vacation.

In the evening my girl friends played softball in the school yard. It was fun to watch them, but I think they sensed that I wanted to get into the game. Of course this was impossible since I could not run. One of the girls came up with an idea that would include me in the game. She suggested that I could take my turn at bat, and if I got a hit another girl would run for me. This really worked out, and I became quite adept at batting. I wanted to try everything.

My father, who never had any lessons in art, was very artistic and loved to draw and paint. We spent hours together with our sketchpads and paints. In school I took advantage of every art class that was offered, and then I would share with my father what I had learned in class. The crafts of sewing, knitting and crocheting were the things my mother was expert in and enjoyed. Although she offered to teach me I had no interest in those things.

My friends all rode bikes and I asked my father to teach me how to ride one. When my mother found out she was against it, afraid that I would fall and get hurt.

"It would be good for her, Ann," my father pointed out to her. "It would build up the strength in her legs."

She finally gave in and even helped us pick out my first bike. On my first attempt to ride, and with my leg so unstable, I found it hard to get on and off the bike. As my mother stood anxiously by I practiced this over and over again. At last I was ready to go, and my father ran along at my side as I circled the block over and over again. He put his hand on my seat and guided me along to make sure I did not fall. Neighbors watched from their front porches and cheered us on. After several weeks I was able to ride alone, though for only short distances, and was able to go riding with my friends.

There was a stable in town where people could ride horses. Uncle Aldo was very athletic and an excellent horseman. He asked me if I would like to learn how to ride, and of course I said yes. Once again, as with the bicycle, there was a problem with my getting on and off, but he figured out a way I could do it. We always picked the smallest horse for me, and I weighed very little for my age. He borrowed a short stepladder and, once I was closer to the saddle, he reached up and guided my body until I was safely on. At first we rode very slowly. As I gained confidence, and Uncle Aldo was sure I would not fall off, we increased our speed. Soon we were racing around the track — experienced horseback riders! We loved these wonderful animals and went riding several times a week. My father sometimes came to watch us, but fortunately my mother never did.

Uncle Aldo taught fencing and water skiing. Both of those sports were obviously not for me. However he had a high-powered speedboat that he loved to race up and down the lake in the summer. His wife, my Aunt Joanne, did not share his enthusiasm for boating, but I did. Although she did not like either swimming or boating, she was also very athletic. In Italy, where she lived until marrying my uncle, she had been a runner-up in track in the Olympics.

Boating and boats had fascinated me ever since I watched them from my window overlooking the lake near Biggs. Sailboats looked like toys from the distance, and I loved watching them. I could also see the long boats being rowed by college students, and sometimes they had races with other colleges. Now that I was home my uncle started taking me on his boat and even let me drive it. Often when I was at the park with my friends he invited them to join us on the boat. Aunt Joanne would watch us from a park bench. Moving fast, whether on a bicycle, a horse, or a speedboat, gave me a marvelous feeling of independence — of freedom. It compensated for having to walk so slowly and never being able to run. I could not wait until I was old enough to get my learner's permit and was already saving for the day I would buy my first car.

On Sundays in the summer my family, along with other relatives and friends, had picnics at the lake. Early on Sunday morning my father went down to the park to reserve and line up picnic tables for our group. This meant that he had to miss going to church, but then he never went anyway. His faith was not as strong as my mother's.

Italian-American picnics are actually feasts, and there was always an unbelievable amount of food. Fresh pasta, meatballs and chicken, roasted potatoes, Italian bread, salads and desserts were placed in picnic baskets and brought to the park. With all of the food we ate somehow I do not remember one single relative as being overweight. Most were quite thin. Apparently it was something in the genes. Once the men had unloaded the cars the women placed tablecloths, silverware, and glasses on the table. There were no paper plates or plastic silverware. It was as fine a table setting as we would have had in our dining rooms at home. While the women took charge of the food, children gathered at the playground. This was something I looked forward to as now I was able to use the swings as well. Following our dinner young families went down to the beach to swim and sunbath. Older relatives just relaxed in the shade and visited. Sometimes the men played cards and drank their homemade wine. Everyone seemed to enjoy these picnics and we were there most of the day.

My parents' best friends, Rose and Carmen Pacelli, lived in Auburn. Both couples had been friends during the Depression and had faced similar hardships. Joanne, their oldest daughter, was my age and became my closest friend. In the summer I was invited to their cottage on Owasco Lake in Auburn. Sometimes I stayed for weeks. Joann had a brother and sister and the four of us had great times together. We swam every day and rowed their large war surplus lifeboat out into the lake. Every day, especially in the summer, I grew stronger. Self-consciousness was soon replaced by self-confidence, hopelessness replaced by happiness, and I was no longer lonely.

* * *

My first real vacation took place when I was fourteen. Our destination was Canada, where my mother and I made a pilgrimage to the shrine of Saint Anne de Beaupre, now a basilica. My father, who never liked to travel or attend church, chose to stay home.

According to Catholic theology, Saint Anne de Beaupre was the mother of Mary and grandmother of Jesus. She was also my mother's patron saint and she believed that this saint, who was said to have performed many miracles, would somehow cure me and overturn the grim prognosis I had been given upon my discharge. Today in Canada and the United States many Catholic families name their daughter Anne. My mother and my daughter are both named Anne.

On our way we visited Montreal and St. Joseph's Oratory, one of the greatest basilicas in the world. It is located on the slope of Mount Royal and from the very top we could see the city of Montreal. St. Joseph's Oratory is a national shrine and is famous for the many cures that supposedly took place there. We also went to Montmorency Falls, which are one and one-half times higher than the Niagara Falls. I loved these falls and, although I did not admit it to my mother, I enjoyed seeing them more than all of the churches we visited along the way. In Quebec we toured some exquisite gardens and again visited more churches. From there we headed towards the shrine of Saint Anne de Beaupre, a short distance from Quebec City. When we arrived our first stop was at the magnificent basilica. Inside the massive doorway on both sides stood huge pyramids of canes, crutches, braces, special shoes, and other things left there by those who had apparently been cured. As I looked up at this unbelievable display left there by the lame and the sick that had benefited from healing miracles, I was in awe. I found myself wondering if these miracles were the same as the miracle I had prayed for years ago at Biggs as I placed my hands on my religious artifacts and asked God for a cure. Were these miracles like the one that my dear friend Elena, who would never be able to make this pilgrimage, prayed for? Why would she have to come here to be cured when she would never be able to make this pilgrimage? She was still at Biggs and getting weaker every day.

According to the teachings of the Catholic Church, a miracle is an extraordinary and astonishing happening that is attributed to the presence and action of an ultimate or divine power. I was determined to find out more about these miraculous cures. After all, that was what my mother had in mind for me when she planned this pilgrimage.

More than a million people visit Saint Anne's every year. When we were there we saw thousands of worshippers. Many were in wheelchairs or on stretchers, others walked with crutches or canes. At night we joined them in an impressive candlelight procession and celebrated Mass in the basilica. In the basement of the basilica we visited the Chapel of the Immaculate Conception and the Chapel of the Blessed Sacrament. Although these two places of worship were small, they were as beautiful as the larger churches we had seen on our journey.

My mother went up the Holy Stairs. Visitors went up these stairs on their knees, but because of the scars on my right knee I was unable to climb them. As I watched her go up slowly on her knees, I knew she was praying for me on every step. I believed that if her prayers were answered I would somehow be cured.

We ate family style in an area where the food was prepared and served by the nuns.

They were very kind, and we enjoyed talking to them.

"Do you know where I might find a book about miracles?" I asked the nun who greeted us at the door.

"Yes, dear, there are many books in the gift shop. I am sure you will find what you are looking for there."

We made our way to the gift shop. While my mother spent time picking up souvenirs for friends and family back home, I found the book section. I found a book that contained stories of people who had been miraculously cured. That night as I read it the thing that stood out to me in the descriptions of the miracles was the fact that none of them were anything you could see. Missing limbs were not replaced, deformities were never made right, scarring never disappeared, and disfigurements and deformities (such as my leg) were never corrected. Then I suddenly realized that my leg would never get longer or larger, my spine would never be straight, my knee would remain atrophic, and the ugly surgical scars would never disappear. There would never be divine intervention for me; I would remain exactly the same for the rest

Another beautiful gown made by my mother for special occasions between 1948 and 1949.

of my life. My mother still had hope that in time Saint Anne would hear her prayers. She clung to her faith and never accepted the scientific information and technology that suggested that these miracles were simply myths, symbols, or illusions.

Shortly after we returned home I got a surprise visit from one of the nurses who had been so wonderful to me at Biggs, Miss Beatrice Gledhill. It was this special person who had spent time with me when she was off duty, and who with her friend Jenny had wheeled me to movies on so many summer evenings. Miss Gledhill had not married and was now director of nurses at Biggs. She offered me a job as her private secretary after graduation. Although I did not accept her kind offer, I did make it a point to stop by and see her on my outpatient visits. Eventually I lost contact with her, as I did with all of my friends at Biggs. My life was different now.

* * *

Growing up I was exposed to the arts and developed a lifelong interest in them. My love of music, concerts, art, museums, and the theater has been ongoing. Writing for the hospital newspapers was a great beginning for the writing I have enjoyed so much over the years. Once I entered public school I discovered how much pleasure I got when speaking in public. At Mynderse one of the requirements for graduation took place in your senior year. Seniors had a choice. They could either take a half-semester course in public speaking, or present a memorized piece at a school assembly. There was no question as to which I would choose, and I was so excited when I spoke in the auditorium in front of the whole school body. I wrote a comedy monologue about a librarian and the various characters she had to deal with in her job. For each character I used a different voice and mannerisms. It was a huge success and, following my presentation, I was invited to perform this monologue for several organizations.

Graduating with honors in the class of 1949 at Mynderse Academy.

In 1949 I graduated from Mynderse Academy with honors, one of the top ten graduating seniors. My parents were very proud of my accomplishments, including all of the awards I had won in the five years that I had been in a real school. The caption under my yearbook picture read, "Versatile Gloria is not only an excellent student but also a fine public speaker and pianist."

It had taken a few years but other than the outpatient visits to Biggs, I had finally made a different life for myself. It was not until after the countless graduation activities that I realized my life was once again going to change. My choice would have been to go right on to college in the fall, but Dr. Severson had other plans for me.

The Fusion

Looking for a college offering a career in the health profession was a top priority in my senior year. However before I made any definite decision about this, Dr. Severson started talking to me about having surgery on my left hip. During an outpatient visit he suggested having the surgery after my graduation from high school and prior to entering college. When he told me that I really needed to consider a surgical fusion of my hip he took me by surprise. Now that I was eighteen years old I didn't have to rely on my parents to find out what this procedure would consist of. This time I would explain it to them. Dr. Severson wanted to have bone grafts made from my healthy bone for use in fusing my hip. This procedure was called arthrodesis and had a great success rate. He had tried for many years to use every conservative method of treatment to immobilize (fuse) my hip, including traction and spica casts. My latest x-rays indicated that nothing had changed since my discharge five years earlier, and with this in mind he strongly urged me to consider this operation. When I asked him how long I would be hospitalized if I agreed to the surgery he told me it would be at least seven or eight months. That was nearly a whole year. This meant that I would not be able to enroll until the following fall.

My first reaction was to refuse. Over the past fourteen years I had had more than enough of hospitals, clinics and doctors. Dr. Severson gave me many reasons why he recommended this fusion. In order to convince me that I should allow this procedure he went over with me again and again the reasons why he strongly recommended it. While doing the fusion he would be able to tip my pelvis. By doing this there was a possibility that I would be able to have a shorter lift.

Entrance to Biggs Memorial Hospital in 1950, with a view of the tower where Peter and I played on the rooftop.

Perhaps I would even be able to walk without the cane that I still used frequently. Once my hip was fused, walking would become so much easier for me and I would not get so fatigued. He was concerned that attending college would be too tiring for me. There would be so much more walking involved than merely walking from room to room as I did in high school. In college I would have to walk from building to building on campus to attend classes. Finally I was told that by having this surgery I would stand a good chance of avoiding severe problems with mobility and constant pain later in life, problems that often were a result of skeletal tuberculosis of the hip. He reminded me that I had my whole life ahead of me, and taking some time off was the right thing to do.

After giving his recommendation a lot of thought, and then talking it over with my parents, I finally gave my consent. Then I just put it in the back of my mind, did not mention it to anyone, and concentrated on graduation. My parents were the only people who knew about my upcoming surgery, and I asked them not to tell anyone about it.

In late September I was once again admitted to Biggs Memorial Hospital, this time three weeks prior to the surgery. According to my chart, this unusually early admission was to be an adjustment period. My days were filled with preoperative testing. Countless x-rays and clinical laboratory tests were done. Blood was also drawn for cross matching in case I required blood transfusions. Clearly this operation was to

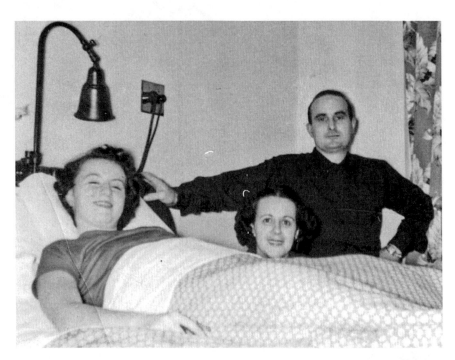

Top: After graduation I returned to Biggs in 1950 for a fusion of my hip. I was there for nearly a year. My parents again are at my bedside. It has been very difficult for them. *Bottom:* A view (top) of the admissions and surgical wards at Biggs in 1950. Women and children's wards are on the lower level.

be a bigger event than I had anticipated. It was obvious that my doctor had played it down when talking to my parents and to me.

There were times when I wished that I had told my friends what was happening. They would have visited me and offered support. My best friend Netta, who is very witty and enjoys humor as much as I do, was the only one I told about my readmission and upcoming surgery. Recently she reminded me that I only confided in her "under penalty of death" if she told anyone. I just could not bring myself to tell my friends or even relatives that I was going back to the sanitarium. Perhaps it was a form of denial. Somehow I would get through it on my own.

On October 13, 1949, one day before my eighteenth birthday, I entered the operating room for the fusion of my left hip. Dr. Severson talked to me again before he performed this second and final surgery for bone tuberculosis on me.

No one had prepared me for what followed. When I woke up from the anesthesia I found myself completely immobilized in yet another spica cast. It was very uncomfortable and felt damp and heavy, bringing back unpleasant memories of casts of the past. Just weeks before I had entered the hospital feeling healthy and energetic. Now I felt so weak and was nauseous for much of the time. One of the medications I was given was so powerful that I lost consciousness. There was a terrifying feeling of falling in space. When I came to I was screaming. Once I had settled down my head began to spin as I thought that I should never have agreed to this—what had I done? This was a very difficult time for me. There was so much pain, and nothing they gave me made it go away. It was excruciating.

After more than a week the pain subsided. In order to assure a complete fusion, I remained in this cast and in a private room on the surgical ward for three long months. Many of my former dreams returned, but now I did not have my childhood dreams of flying over rooftops— playing with the happy children. My dreams were different now, as you can tell from this poem that I wrote.

"Dreams"

> I sleep
> walking, running, jumping,
> arms outstretched.
> facing upward towards the sky.
> Floating over rooftops, mountains, lakes.
> Feeling free, free from pain, and falling.
> I wake, sitting up slowly, feeling pain.

I reach for my crutches, moving slowly,
afraid of falling, careful steps.
My body imprisoned.
Never free, always me.

*   *   *

One day, several weeks before Christmas, the hospital director came to my room and told me I had been chosen to be interviewed for the radio station WHCU Ithaca. This local station had a program called Hometown Story, a regular Sunday afternoon feature. The interview took place and was broadcast live right in my room. A reporter asked me questions about the illness that I had had for so many years and how, despite my handicap, I had managed to attend school and graduate from high school. The object of this program was to push the sale of Christmas seals. It was an honor for me to be asked to participate and to share my story. Others present at the time of the interview were the hospital director, Dr. Stanley N. Lincoln, as well as a member of both the board of directors of the Tompkins County TB and Public Health Association and the Tompkins County Visitors Service. Board members also asked me questions. When asked if I had done any Christmas shopping I told them that I was in the process of making everyone gifts with the assistance of the occupational therapist at the hospital. On the day of the interview my relatives gathered at my parents' house and tuned in to the program. When an Ithaca newspaper printed this story I proudly presented my parents with the copy that had been mailed to me. Although I have been interviewed by radio reporters many times in my life, that is the one that is the most memorable.

Getting through the holidays was very hard for me. Instead of sharing Thanksgiving dinner with family and friends, I had a tray delivered to my room. It was the typical holiday dinner, with turkey and pumpkin pie, but it was not the same as the delicious food my family always prepared. There had been too many Christmases away from home, not just for me but for my parents as well. Since returning home I had loved the wonderful holiday traditions and celebrations. It was a magical time, shared with our large families and many friends. Now that I was older, my mother asked if I would not mind if they visited me on the day before Christmas. I knew how much she wanted to spend the holiday with her family and Maryann, who was now eleven years old, and I really did not blame her. They had given up so much for me, and this was my chance to do something for them. My sister would not be able to visit me even

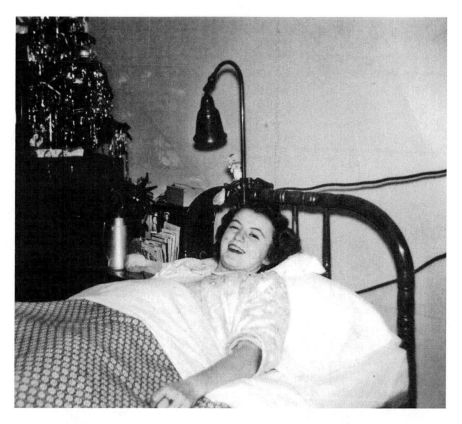

Another Christmas away from home in 1950. My entering college has been on hold for a year.

on the holiday because of the strict hospital rules. Although I said it would be all right, I really did not look forward to spending this holiday alone in my private room. This was the first Christmas that I was not with my parents; they had always come to whatever hospital I was in.

My father placed a small tree with festive ornaments and tiny lights in my room. They brought many brightly wrapped gifts for me, including gifts from my relatives. All of these were piled high on the stand next to my bed. They held no interest for me, but I never let my parents know this. Instead I laughed and exchanged jokes with my father as I opened each present. In the morning as I looked at the beautiful little tree and pile of gifts I felt so sad, so alone. We were all served special meals that day, but I was overcome by a wave of depression and could not eat anything. The staff did everything to make this day enjoyable for us. One of my favorite orderlies, David, was dressed as Santa Claus and passed out candy and other treats for us. When he came near me I reached over and pulled down his beard.

"I knew it was you, David," I laughed. "Merry Christmas!"

A young man passed my room every week when he came to visit his sister who was recuperating from lung surgery. On Christmas day he noticed that I had no visitors, and he stopped in and introduced himself. It was so good to talk to someone my age, and soon he made it a practice to spend some time with me when he came to see his sister. Then he started bringing me flowers and kissing me just before he left. Naturally I was flattered by his attention, but I did not have any romantic feelings for him. All I wanted was a friend. Then around the time I was scheduled to be transferred to the other part of the building he started getting serious. One day he showed up with a tiny black jewelry box. He opened it up so that I could see the beautiful little diamond ring inside. He asked me to marry him. It was unreal — he had never even seen me out of my bed, and I had done nothing to encourage him. He knew about my plan to attend college the following year. When I told him I could not accept the ring I was careful to explain that my feeling towards him was one of friendship and that I was not in love with him. It did not surprise me that he never came to see me again.

Next I started getting visits from the in-house Romeos, checking out the young women on the floor. One of the young men, Michael, was just a year older than I was and had pulmonary tuberculosis. In addition to being rather good looking, he had a wonderful sense of humor and a very positive attitude about his illness. We were attracted to one another and he visited me every day. Plans were made to attend events in the auditorium together once I was back in a wheelchair and transferred to another floor. It appeared we would soon be carrying on the sanitarium tradition of cousining.

*   *   *

During the five years I had been away from the sanitarium the first lasting cure for tuberculosis was discovered by Selman A. Waksman, an expert in the field of microbiology. Following years of research this anti-tuberculosis ("wonder drug") streptomycin was introduced and was administered for the first time to a critically ill tuberculosis patient. The immediate effects were astonishing as the patient's advanced disease was visibly arrested, the bacteria disappeared from his sputum, and he made a rapid recovery. This new drug had some side effects, but it was used successfully and was soon followed by many other anti–TB drugs. It was not long, however, before streptomycin-resistant tubercle bacilli appeared. Scientists discovered that giving combinations of these drugs worked better than using just one.

Some of the patients I visited with on the surgical floor told me stories about people they knew who had been completely cured after receiving streptomycin. They also told me that there were some side effects from taking streptomycin, especially on the inner ear. These caused hearing loss and problems in balance. Still everyone I talked to seemed to agree that the positive effects of this drug far outweighed its problems.

I spent many months as a patient on the surgical ward recuperating from my operation. In talking to other patients I found out about the different surgeries and other procedures that were performed there. Sometimes the treatments were unsuccessful and had to be repeated. It was a very stressful time for them as they went through this stage of their cure. When their test results indicated that they had improved they were transferred to an ambulatory floor.

As a child I witnessed the disfigurement of the chest of several patients who had undergone lung surgery for pulmonary tuberculosis. It was a terrible sight and one that I have never forgotten. When they talked about going through a procedure called pneumothorax, I did not really understand what it was all about. Now I was about to find out.

Artificial pneumothorax (lung collapse) was the first surgical procedure for tuberculosis and the most common form of medical intervention in this country from the 1930s through the 1950s. In this procedure anesthesia was injected into the pleural cavity. Surgeons then made a small incision, inserted a needle, and connected it to a machine. Filtered air or nitrogen was injected into the pleural cavity to press against the tubercular lung and prevent its movement. Over the next few weeks the pleural cavity was filled progressively and then additional refills were given periodically to maintain the collapse. If successful, pneumothorax often relieved symptoms that included cough, fever, spitting up, and lack of appetite. A popular theory was that it also reduced the number of toxins produced by the bacteria.

Pneumothorax was a dangerous and very painful treatment, and often surgeons dealt with accidental puncturing of the lung and adhesions. For this reason it was usually done only on those who had advanced disease and who did not respond to other types of therapy. If this procedure could not be done surgeons often performed an extrapleural pneumothorax. In this invasive surgery part of the rib was removed so that they could push the lung in. After closing they were then able to collapse the lung by putting air into the space the same way they did with the artificial pneumothorax. Thoracoplasty was used whenever it was impossible to do pneumothorax. It soon became the surgery of choice worldwide. This major surgery not only reduced chest deformity, but was permanent.

A collapsed lung at rest healed more quickly than a working lung, even though the working one was kept at a minimum of work by complete bed rest at the beginning of the cure. Sometimes spontaneous pneumothorax occurred when lungs rotted and collapsed. Bilateral pneumothorax consisted of the compression of both lungs by this method. Adhesions were often cauterized between the chest wall and the lung (pneumonolysis), as they prevented satisfactory collapse of the lung. Phrenectomy consisted of a division or crushing of the phrenic nerve that moves the diaphragm up and down while breathing.

Other major surgical procedures included pneumonectomy, where the entire affected lung was removed, or lobectomy, the partial removal of an infected lobe. In addition to x-rays doctors often used instruments called fluoroscopes or bronchoscopes to view the chest.

As I talked to patients recuperating as I was from surgery, I felt such compassion for what they were going through. People on this surgical unit were very sick. Although I found their stories interesting, they were very depressing. I was trying so hard to stop my own bouts of depression and could not wait to be moved to another ward.

*   *   *

Eventually as I gained strength and started to feel better I was transferred to D-1, the ambulatory women's floor where I had been placed after H building closed years ago. I shared a room with Barbara, a high school student who hoped to be home in time to graduate the following year. There was a strong possibility that this would not happen as she had tuberculosis of her spine. We remained roommates until I was discharged more than six months later.

Even though the operation itself was successful, the road to recovery was not an easy one. Doctors began removing parts of my cast, a little at a time, so that I could start learning how to walk all over again. My hip was fused, my pelvis was tilted, and every step was painful. Because of my tipped pelvis, my lift, although still more than five inches high, would be slightly shorter on my next pair of shoes. There are few people with a lift this high that can walk without any assistance, back pain, or a pronounced limp.

Every day as I walked slowly on my crutches down the long corridor fellow patients would cheer me on from their rooms. It reminded me of the times my neighbors at home had cheered my father and me on as I circled the block on my bicycle. It really helped to have this kind of support. Not exactly the Olympics, but just a wonderful feeling of accomplishment once I reached the finish line at the end of the ward. As always, I was aiming for the gold.

It was not long before the entire cast was removed and I was able to walk without crutches or canes for the first time since I was five years old. Would this be my last cast, my last surgery, my last confinement? Only time would tell if this was the end of my long battle with bone tuberculosis.

Although I had not wanted to return to Biggs, I found it very easy to fall into the familiar routines I had grown up with. Even though I now looked at things differently, I found myself once again getting very involved in sanitarium life. At home I had never had a date, just painful crushes on several of the boys at school. I am sure most young people go through this at some time, but in my case I really believed I would never be asked out. It was different at Biggs, and I think one of the main reasons was that I was more relaxed and less timid there. Just as we had planned, Michael and I started going everywhere and doing things together. Perhaps if they had a formal dance here I might have even had a chance to be a princess on the court — or a queen riding in her chariot — or wheelchair. Barbara was confined to her bed and relied on me to tell her what was going on outside of our room. She became my confidant and looked forward to hearing about every detail of my dates with Michael. These included having meals with him in the dining hall, attending movies and shows in the auditorium, making things together in occupational therapy, and disappearing into the many hiding places of the building where we could make out — the more innocent version of cousining. When I told Michael about Barbara he made it a point to visit her when he came to pick me up. Sometimes the three of us played cards and board games. Michael was discharged shortly afterwards. We made promises to each other which we never kept.

It was not long before I started seeing Patrick, an interesting man who had recently graduated from law school. Shortly after passing his bar examinations he had been diagnosed with pulmonary tuberculosis and admitted to Biggs. Although I enjoyed being with him, he was much older than I was. It was not the same as being with Michael, and we never became "cousins."

I met Robbie in occupational therapy. He looked much older than his actual age, which I guessed to be mid-twenties. Robbie had been a patient at Biggs for years. Every time his laboratory and x-ray tests were normal he was told he would be discharged soon, but he never was. Instead he suffered many relapses as the persistent germs attacked his lungs again and again. Then he had to start his long cure all over again. Like so many others that this happened to, he often became depressed. It was too much for him to cope with.

Robbie had a reputation for making the most exquisite jewelry. Patients were encouraged to enter the things they made in local fairs and other craft events, where they could sell them or compete for prizes. He was always a winner, taking first prize for his jewelry. We became good friends and he knew how much I admired the necklaces he made. One day he presented me with a small box. I opened it eagerly to find a magnificent necklace with an acrylic pendant with a tiny rose bud embedded inside. It was lovely, and I wore it all the time. We talked about what we were going to do when we were discharged. I told him about my plans for college. He had been at Biggs for so long that he was not sure what he would do. Before he was admitted he had worked in a jewelry store, but he doubted that he would get that same job back. Perhaps he too would apply to college.

When Robbie stopped coming to occupational therapy I asked one of the therapists where he was. Had he been discharged without saying goodbye? I was told that he had been transferred to C-2 for surgery. When I visited him there while he was recuperating from his operation I could not believe how ill he was. He lay there on his bed, pale and lifeless. Somehow he managed a weak smile as he looked at me with such sad eyes. It was not long after that we learned that he had passed away. It was weeks before I was able to enter the occupational therapy rooms again, but I still wore my beautiful necklace every day.

In the evenings men and women from D-1 and E-1 gathered in the large day room near the auditorium. Although I had enjoyed this room on my prior admission, it was so much more fun now that I was older. It was definitely the part of my day that I looked forward to the most.

Television was new then and we all were very excited when one was put into this room. There were very few channels and it was all in black and white. There was nothing on that I cared to watch. Still we were all intrigued by this new technology, and the men especially enjoyed the wrestling. Since I had taken piano lessons at home, I was now able to play either the upright piano in the day room, or the grand piano in the auditorium. Although I still did not like to play in front of an audience, I loved playing the easy pieces David had taught me when no one was around.

At night couples often wandered down to the vacant corridors located at the end of the center of the building. This was where maintenance and storage rooms were situated. They were always closed at night but never locked. There was no supervision or members of the staff checking that area. It was the ideal place for couples to be alone and to participate in whatever stage of cousining they were in.

Time went by very quickly with so much to do. Much of my time was spent reading, and I spent countless hours in the library. My favorite pastime was writing for the hospital paper and reporting the news of the floor I was on. Every month I tried to make the column more interesting and I soon found that when I used humor the readers seemed to like it more. My writing was a stress reliever for them. Was it sometimes ridiculous? Of course. A stress reliever? You bet. Did it make them laugh? Definitely. Was this the beginning of my future career as a comedy writer? Absolutely not!

* * *

At the request of one of the teachers I helped teach history to those patients doing work at the high school level. This was very challenging to me, but once I organized a study plan I became completely absorbed with it. My students seemed to enjoy my teaching, or was it because I never gave them tests or homework?

Along with a fellow patient, John, I hosted an in-house radio show, the Musical Caravan. This was the same two-hour broadcast that I had been an announcer for as a child. This show featured a variety of music on phonograph records, most of which had been donated by patients and staff. We cranked out tunes from the tiny broadcasting studio and played requests whenever possible. Our listening audience increased when John, during an unsuccessful attempt to adjust the phonograph, started swearing in frustration. He had forgotten to disconnect and everyone heard him. Needless to say he took a lot of teasing after that incident, but our show was not banned by the medical staff or, as we liked to call them, the network bosses.

Barbara and I were never ready to sleep at the time when lights and radios had to be turned off. Since our ward ran parallel to C-1 and C-2, we decided it would be fun to purchase flashlights and send signals after dark. It was not long before we started getting signals back. This went on until one of the floor night nurses turned us in. She considered herself the captain of the night patrol. One of the men on C-2 figured out which room was using flashlights. When he was transferred to an ambulatory ward he tracked us down and introduced himself, and the three of us became good friends. We laughed as we recalled our short-lived flashing adventure.

There were some brave souls on the men's ambulatory ward that were much more adventurous than we were. Years earlier I had read about their escapades in the hospital newspapers. Since their ward was also located on the ground floor it was easy for them to climb out of their windows after dark and climb into the windows of women they knew on D-1. These evening rendezvous usually took place when the weather was warm and were prearranged so that the Juliets could unlock their windows ahead of time to let their Romeos in. Fortunately there were no balconies involved. Even more daring were those young men who walked up to the main highway at night, usually on the weekend, and hitchhiked into Ithaca. They went to local bars and dances, often at one of the college campuses, and according to all reports, had a very good time. This became a very serious problem. First of all they were not only putting themselves at risk, but the general public as well. Since these were young men they were able to fit right into this college town, easily passing themselves off as students. If anyone got caught they were given a warning, and privileges were taken away if they were caught again. They were also told that if they continued to do this they would be asked to leave the institution, even though they were not cured. Their friends at Biggs were warned not to tell anyone of their excursions. We all talked and laughed when we heard about their escapades, but we also realized how foolish they were to risk the possibility of never getting well or making others sick.

In the spring I couldn't wait to revisit the picnic area and trails where I had spent so much time after learning to use crutches for the first time. Sometimes I went there alone and sat by myself, enjoying the stillness and beauty surrounding me. At other times I went there with a boyfriend, or with other friends. We sometimes brought a picnic bag lunch which the kitchen staff was kind enough to prepare for us. It was a serene, peaceful haven for all of us lucky enough to be there.

*　*　*

On one of the monthly orthopedic visits Dr. Severson did not come. Instead he sent one of his assistants. For weeks I had been anxiously awaiting this visit because I felt I was doing so well. Gradually I had been able to discard the crutches and just use a cane. Prior to the surgery I had practically eliminated using a cane, except for unusually long walks. Now I wanted to know if I could eliminate the cane entirely and start walking on my own. When I asked this young resident he just shook his head and told me emphatically that I could not stop using a cane. He also said I would have to use a cane all of the time for the rest of my life. When he told me that I became very upset. After all I had gone through I did not expect this, and I overreacted to what he told me. I grabbed my cane and threw it across the room. By now, unlike most patients, I was not intimidated by doctors. Usually the people I knew rarely questioned them and just accepted whatever they said. That was not me, and I yelled at him hysterically, "I will walk out of here on my own two feet and without a cane if it is the last thing I do."

He just shrugged his shoulders, wrote something down on my chart, and without a word left the room. After that incident I worked even harder, pacing myself slowly as I took a few steps at a time each day without using the cane. A month later Dr. Severson was back and he was amazed at my progress. He never mentioned the incident with his resident, and told me that I could now eliminate using the cane completely unless I found walking tiring. It was time to go home. I asked him what I could expect in the future.

Ambulatory patients playing croquet in the summer of 1951.

Above: Arnie and I are finalists in the croquet tournament and are awaiting our turn. *Left:* A final goodbye with my friend Leo in 1951.

It would be just as hard to leave this time as it had been before. Like many patients about to be discharged, I did not really want to leave. Once I had left the surgical floor I had fallen into a comfortable routine and started to truly enjoy myself. My Biggs family for the past eight months had given me so much joy. They were from all walks of life and had shared with me their stories of the past and their hopes for the future. How I dreaded the phone call from home telling me what day my parents would be coming to take me home.

The call came on one of those beautiful warm summer evenings when I was outside playing croquet with my friends. An orderly came outside to tell me that I had a phone call. It was my mother. I actually felt sick to my stomach as I listened to her. She was overjoyed and told me exactly when they would be picking me up.

Once again on the day I was discharged I said my good-byes to everyone. There was both laughter and tears as I embraced my friends and members of the staff. Now I had just a few months to reunite with my friends at home. I had not been in contact with them for nearly a year. It would be hard. Still, I looked forward to seeing them, and to seeing the look on their faces when they saw how much better I could now walk.

My outpatient visits would

On the day of my discharge from Biggs in 1951 Elena and I have our picture taken. We were both in tears as I left with my parents to return home once again.

continue for another year. At the time of discharge, and for the first time in fourteen years, I was able to walk without any assistance. Now that the surgery had made it possible for me to have a slightly shorter lift, I had to have it adjusted. I still had a slight limp and was unable to walk or run at a fast pace, but at least I could walk! Every conservative and operative method of treatment had been given to me in this seemingly endless battle that finally ended in my eighteenth year.

When I was first discharged from Biggs in 1944 my prognosis was "good for life but poor for recovery from the disease." Prognosis on this final discharge appeared on my chart as "good for life and good for recovery from the disease."

*   *   *

At home I went through another period of depression, although it was not as severe as the one following my previous discharge. Everything changed forever once I left the sanitarium, and once again it took awhile to readjust. Being hospitalized even for such a short time changed the way I felt about myself, about my life. Sometimes one of my parents drove me to the hospital and waited in the car while I visited my friends. These visits were always in the evening during the week, when I knew my friends would not have other visitors. Once I entered the hospital and walked down the long corridor towards their ward I realized that I had forgotten just how quiet it was there at night. It was so unlike the busy home and neighborhood where I now lived. I continued these visits all through the summer, but then I did not return for many years. How I wish I had kept in touch with my friends there, but I was too caught up in my own life and I needed to put that part of my life behind me.

Getting reunited with my friends at home helped somewhat. They invited me to join them for a week at a small cottage on the lake. Although I think they never really understood why I had not told them about my second trip to Biggs, it was never mentioned. I never discussed anything about my surgery or my experiences at the hospital with anyone.

My father was forced into early retirement when the factory where he was employed as core maker closed. He was never able to find a job that he liked so he tried different things. For a short period of time he went into a small business with my Uncle Peps (Joseph) selling used items. During the summer he worked outdoors at Cayuga Lake State Park. He never found a full-time job again. When my mother quit her job at the New York Shop she opened up her own business in our home selling women's clothes. Her father and two of her brothers, Uncle Mario and Uncle Lee, now had their own business— M. Giovannini and Sons. They built a large addition on our house for the dress shop. My father now claimed he had more than enough to do helping her out. He loved to tell people, "Now instead of working forty hours a week I am working sixty!"

Of course he was exaggerating. His sense of humor was like that of Elena's, and we all enjoyed his quick wit and droll manner. As my mother's business grew she bought a small building downtown and moved her exquisite dress shop there. We were so proud of her as owner of the Anne Didio Dress Shop.

We went on another pilgrimage to the shrine at St. Anne's. This time my mother's parents went with us. I did not look for a miracle this time, although I am sure they all did. It was my belief that those who claimed to regain their sight, hearing, and ability to walk, and to have had internal tumors and pain disappear simply had enough faith to heal themselves through the powers of their minds. I did not have that faith. My miracle was that I had survived my disability both emotionally and physically, and that I had been left with the strength and determination to lead a normal life.

As I sat in the outpatient clinic at Biggs for what was to be my final appointment with Dr. Severson I was very nervous. After examining me he reviewed the results of the latest x-rays of my fused hip and told me that everything looked good. He then proceeded to tell me what I could expect in the future. I did not like what he told me. Eventually, he explained, the wear and tear on my tilted spine, combined with the considerable difference in the length of my legs, would gradually affect my mobility. This would no doubt lead to my having to be permanently in a wheelchair by the age of forty. He went on to tell me that if I got married and became pregnant it would be wise to consider having only one child. It would be too much of a strain on my back, both during pregnancy and afterward when I was lifting and caring for my child. His recommendation was that if I should became pregnant I should consider having a cesarean section in order to protect not only the baby but my fused hip as well. I said nothing. I could not catch my breath. We shook hands as he wished me luck and I returned home. I refused to believe what he had told me, and made up my mind that I would do everything possible to prove him wrong. Over the years I did just that.

The College Years

Without any help from a school guidance counselor or my parents, and with very little knowledge about colleges in general, I started looking for a small college. No one in my family had ever gone to college. I was the first. My choice was one that was not too far from home in Alfred, New York. This rural village is situated in a high valley at the foothills of the Allegheny Mountains. It is home to two schools, Alfred University, a private institution; and Alfred State College (SUNY Alfred), a highly regarded division of the State University of New York. These colleges face each other across the valley. SUNY Alfred, the college I attended, is located on the upper campus. This location presented yet another problem for me in the months that followed.

Since I had not visited Alfred before and had seen few pictures of it, I had never imagined that it would be so picturesque. Houses and buildings in this tiny village blended right in with the college campus. There were several large homes in the village that had been converted into residences for students. All meals were served in the dining room, although everyone had the option of eating in the cafeteria on campus. Each house was managed by a housemother. There were many rules to follow, but only one that we objected to. This was the one, carefully monitored by our housemother, which stated that boys were never to come inside of the house. On the evenings when any one of her girls was returning to the house after a date she made sure that the boys did not get past the front steps where the anticipated good night kiss often took place. Some of the boys often made fun of her and, when she could not hear them, called her the warden or keeper

I wore this dress at my first formal dance at college in 1952.

of the keys. But to us she was simply a kind lady who took very good care of us.

At Alfred I was even more self-conscious of my disability than I was when I entered school at Mynderse. It seemed like I was the only one on campus with a visible disability, and I struggled with the challenges it presented. In the fall I was able to walk from the house to my classes on the hill while at the same time carrying my books. Although many of my housemates had the same classes that I did I always started out earlier and walked alone so that I would not slow them down. Finally they would catch up to me, laughing and talking and sometimes offering to carry my books. It was the same when we walked home for lunch, but I finally had to give up on that. For the entire time I attended school there

I ate my lunch in the cafeteria on campus. It was not much different than when I was at Mynderse and ate alone in my home room while others walked home for lunch. It was so hard not to feel different, and I was becoming increasingly frustrated. It did not help when two fraternity brothers walked by me and I heard them laugh and make rude remarks about my gait and my granny shoes. No one at home or in school had ever ridiculed me for being disabled. Tears streamed down my face, and I became more withdrawn than ever after that incident.

What got me through the first few months was the fulfillment and feeling of accomplishment in my classes, and the fact that my grades were outstanding. Sometimes my friends would tease me about always keeping lists, which I have continued to this day, and being so dedicated to my work. However it became a regular routine for them to gather around my desk the night before an important examination and ask me to review my class notes that I had organized on a daily basis.

My social life was not as fulfilling as my academic one. A combination of the effects of skeletal tuberculosis and a lack of self-confidence, especially in social situations, resulted in my rarely being asked out on a date. My first blind date was an absolute nightmare. A girlfriend had arranged a double date for us. During the course of the evening I overheard her speaking softly to him, apologizing that she had picked me for the date. I was crushed, and I began to wonder how many other students were whispering unkind things about me behind my back. It was hard to accept the fact that they treated me differently when I so desperately wanted to be one of them. Despite this incident the seven of us, who were in the same class, taking similar courses, and living in the same house, became close friends. We all agreed to pledge the same sorority. Some of us were invited to join, but when we found out the others were not we decided to stay where we were. At any rate everyone seemed to be more interested in the social activities of the fraternities. It was not too long after this that I starting dating a boy from one of the fraternities. Here again I started making lists—this time of fraternity parties.

One morning in November I woke up to find a blanket of snow covering the village. It was breathtaking and the whole campus looked like a winter wonderland. As I started walking to class I lifted my head and opened my mouth to catch some snowflakes on my tongue. Then I suddenly fell on the slippery sidewalk. For the next few weeks I tried desperately to walk to class, but it was often impossible and I missed many classes. There was no parent to put me on a sled and slide me up the hills. In desperation I called my parents and asked them to come and get me. It had all become too much for me and I wanted them to bring me home. I was so tired.

When they arrived we met with my advisor. He encouraged me to stay in school and told my parents how well I was doing in my classes. When he started pointing out all of the advantages of the college I became angry and said, "What good is all of this when I cannot walk on the campus or get to my classes?"

I have never forgotten asking that question, fighting back tears, as my parents remained silent. They simply did not know what to say or how to cope with this unforeseen development in my life. My advisor apologized and said he had not realized what a hard time I was having.

This was in the 1950s when there were no mandates to provide access for disabled students. It would be years before the civil rights movement for people with disabilities began, and it was not until 1990 when the ADA (Americans with Disabilities Act) would go into effect.

My advisor told us not to worry and assured us that the college would somehow work out a plan to provide transportation for me to and from my classes. As my parents looked at me anxiously I kept thinking about what I had asked of them. I was sorry that I had asked them to make the long trip. I could not bear to see them so unhappy.

That is when I made the decision to give the advisor's plan a try and remain in school. Within days I was told that arrangements had been made with one of the fraternities to bring me from and to classes. A schedule had been given to them, and I was to call if there were any changes in my schedule. This was such a relief to me, and I took great pleasure in the fact that I was now the envy of my roommates. Instead of feeling sorry for me they looked at me in awe as every day a car driven by one of many fraternity brothers came for me. They were some of the best-looking and popular boys on campus. I will be forever grateful to these young men, so unlike the two who had upset me weeks before. They were all volunteers. When the weather was especially icy they would get out of the car, gallantly take my books my arm, and escort me to class. Did I now feel self-conscious? Not at all, I was actually enjoying this daily routine. It did not matter to me if the cold icy weather never ended. And yes, I did make out yet another list.

It was at this time, especially after having the luxury of car rides to classes, that I started thinking about learning how to drive and purchasing a car. This would give me the independence I so longed for. It was then that I decided to develop a plan for accomplishing this.

Before the summer break I took and passed a federal government civil service test. Once the term ended and I had returned home I went to the personnel office at Sampson Air Force Base, a training center for the air force located just twenty miles from my house. When I presented my test results along with my typing certificates for speed I was offered a well-paying job as private secretary to the flight surgeon and his staff of doctors. Flight surgeons are military medical doctors who are primarily responsible for the medical evaluation, health and preventative care for the personnel stationed at the base. Generally they are not surgeons and do not operate. I did not mention the fact that I was enrolled in college and would be returning there when the fall term started. It was all part of the plan.

This job was very interesting and I learned so much about the military and the history of our armed forces. And it was such fun! Every morning basic trainees dressed in fatigues marched behind their drill sergeant singing the familiar chants, usually about the opposite sex. As they marched past the office I could look out of the window and hear their humorous and often risqué chants. Some of them went something like this: "I've got a gal who's mighty willin', now she's takin' penicillin." And another one which went "I know a girl who lives on the hill. She won't do it but her sister will." They would end these chants shouting the familiar "Sound off, sound off." My housemother would have been horrified, and my own mother as well!

As summer drew to a close I began to wonder if I should stay there instead of returning to Alfred. There was very little walking required in this job, and the pay and benefits were outstanding. Everyone, including the flight surgeon, encouraged me to stay. It was tempting, but in the end I decided to return to school.

During my senior year in college I wrote my thesis on tuberculosis of the bones and joints, using my own case history as an example. Up until that time everything I knew about tuberculosis was based on my own personal experiences. Over the years I learned so much about this disease from listening to the conversations and concerns of other patients, watching the progression of their cures, and constantly asking them questions. Our hospital newspapers also provided interesting articles about the disease. Eventually I learned much more about my own particular form of this debilitating disease.

In order to write my thesis I made a trip to Biggs to get permission from the director, Dr. Stanley N. Lincoln, to have my medical records released to me. These records consisted of two huge volumes, with hundreds of pages that gave detailed information about every aspect of my cure. It was fortunate that I was able to obtain them at that time because it was not long before all patient records that had been saved for so many years were destroyed. In school I found most of the science classes, and chemistry in particular, fascinating, although the most interesting one was microbiology.

I became involved in many campus activities and the time went by very fast. As the social editor of the student newspaper I wrote a column, "Night and Day," about the social events on campus. It was well received. I gradually started adding humor to it just as I had as a child when writing my "Small Fry" column for the hospital newspaper.

Another elective course I took at Alfred was public speaking. Once I completed this course I used every opportunity to speak before groups of people. Now I was beginning to have more and more self-confidence. When I was asked to be the keynote speaker at the annual banquet for seniors I was overjoyed. This was an honor that I had hoped for but never imagined I would get. It would have been quite simple to just follow the content of previous presentations in which the chosen speaker reflected on the joys of the college and the wonderful professors and people in charge of residences. I decided to take it in another direction and presented a humorous piece that poked fun at the college, the staff and the curriculum. Of course my concluding words were serious and well thought out. After all, I wanted to graduate! After the banquet my favorite professor, who taught my favorite subject, microbiology, came up to me and said, "My goodness, Gloria, I never knew you had that in you. You were always so quiet in class."

For my graduation many of my relatives from both sides of my family came. I was the first one to get a college degree. When I walked up to the podium to receive my diploma summa cum laude, a proud member of the Phi Theta Kappa Arts and Sciences Honor Society, I spotted my parents in the front row.

This is for you, I thought, as I raised my diploma.

At the party following the graduation ceremony, my mother was talking to our housemother. She thanked my mother for inviting my group of friends to Seneca Falls the previous weekend. They had told her what a wonderful time they had at Gloria's home. Actually they had never been invited or gone to my home. Instead we had signed out for there, but had made previous arrangements to camp out in a park nearby. We let some of our friends, including boys, know where we would be. To my relief my mother just nodded her head, and then managed a weak smile as our housemother went on about the trip. When our house-mother looked at us and winked, we realized that she must have known about our plans all along.

As for my mother, who was an extremely outgoing women who loved adventures, she never mentioned mine to me. She was one of a kind.

Continuing Changes

Once I was settled in at home I returned to Sampson Air Force Base and applied for a job in the clinical laboratory at the hospital. This 1,500-bed hospital was located in another section of the government complex, apart from where basic training took place. It was the largest air force hospital in the country and met the health needs of military personnel, including the thousand of basic trainees. The Seneca Army Airfield was located nearby and servicemen who needed to be hospitalized were brought here.

Sampson Air Force Base was located on the eastern shore of Seneca Lake in the Finger Lakes region of upstate New York. It had originally been built as a military training ground for the navy. People in the area were very excited when this base was built and welcomed navy personnel with open arms. My friends and I were too young to date the sailors stationed there, but we did manage to get navy double-breasted pea coats just like theirs. Some even topped it off with a white sailor's cap. Sampson Naval Base was primarily used during World War II and closed when the war ended. It was a sad day for the area since the base had stimulated the economy and provided many jobs. Eventually we stopped wearing our pea coats.

During the Korean War the base was reopened as a basic training base for the air force. After rotating through all of the departments I was assigned to the microbiology laboratory. Since tuberculosis is a bacterial disease, it was there under the microscope that I finally met the enemy, tiny microscopic rods called *Mycobacterium tuberculosis*. These powerful tiny warriors had invaded my body and changed my life.

In the laboratory we were able to isolate and identify tubercle bacilli from samples of sputum and other body fluids. We made a special media that contained nutrients that these bacilli thrived on. This media was placed in large glass tubes. If these life-threatening organisms were present they multiplied and grew in yellow colonies, looking rather innocuous on the pale green medium.

Sampson offered many workshops and lectures for those in my field. We also had the opportunity to take college courses nearby, and I took advantage of both.

Throughout my career I worked in several different hospitals, where I spent much of the time working in the fascinating world of microorganisms.

*   *   *

With so many service men stationed at this base it was no wonder that they started dating women who lived in this rural area. They met many of them who had jobs at the base or the hospital. Courtships, engagements and marriages increased dramatically. Because I was actually working on the base, and had constant contact with many of these men, some of my friends started asking me if I could arrange blind dates for them. Two of the couples that I introduced ended up getting married. I was the Italian American Yenta.

Married couples either lived in housing on the base or in the towns nearby. When an airman was transferred to another base, the couple had to move. There were parents who understandingly worried about their daughters marrying men that they knew little or nothing about. This was how my parents felt, but I did not listen to them.

One day a fine-looking

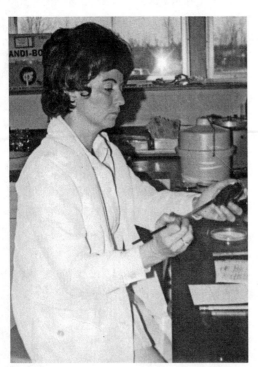

My first job in the microbiology department at the Sampson Air Force Base hospital, Romulus, New York, in 1953.

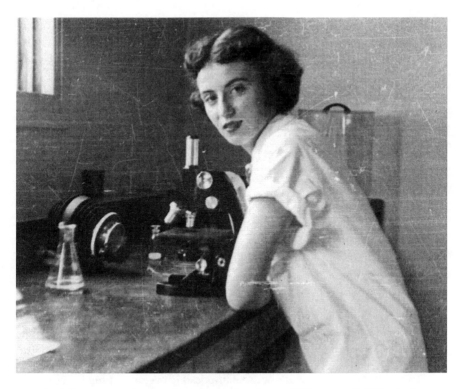

In the laboratory, using a microscope, I study specially stained slides, looking for the bacilli that cause tuberculosis.

young staff sergeant walked in to our secretary's office and handed her his papers. He had just been transferred to Sampson and assigned to the laboratory. When he left I told the secretary, "That is the man I am going to marry," and a few months later I did. Shortly after our marriage we learned that plans had been made to close the base. We moved to New Haven, Connecticut, where my husband had been transferred. Because I was a civil service government employee I soon obtained a job in a nearby hospital for veterans. One year later our son, Stephen Michael, was born. Although I had my prenatal care with a civilian obstetrician in New Haven, the military insurance would not cover hospitalization there. Instead I had no choice but to go to the nearest air force hospital once I went into labor. There were a number of officers there who were obstetricians. None of them had ever seen or examined me. They were concerned about my delivery because of my fused hip. I overheard them talking as they consulted with one another about the best way to deliver my baby. Should they have me lay on my side? Which side, left or right? Should I have a cesarean section? I was already exhausted from the eighty-mile trip and intense labor pains. It was quite a shock to everyone who worked on the maternity ward to learn that the doctors decided to ask the Chief of Surgery to deliver my baby. This was unheard of. This doctor was an air force colonel as well as a board-certified GYN/OB specialist. When this doctor examined me he immediately took charge, had me lay on my back, assured me that I had nothing to worry about, and went on with a perfectly normal delivery. Stephen Michael was placed in my arms, and as I looked at him I thought he was the most beautiful baby I had ever seen. It was one of the happiest moments in my life. A few years later my husband was discharged and we returned to Seneca Falls. My mother had been right all along, and it was not long before he left the area, leaving me and my son. We never heard from him again.

* * *

I had to find a job in order to support us so I went to work in the laboratory of Taylor-Brown Memorial Hospital, a small hospital just minutes away from Seneca Falls. I was offered full-time employment, which I tried for a while. There was a serious shortage of laboratory personnel but full-time work became impossible because of my fatigue and weakness in my leg. Instead I decided to work permanent part-time. This turned out to be a good decision because I really needed to spend more time with my son. The laboratory was closed at night so everyone who worked there was required to take turns being on emergency call. Sometimes I was called out during the night and did not get home until daybreak. After several years it became too much for me and I had to withdraw. I felt bad because the other technicians then had to fill my schedule. My co-workers were very understanding. We were like a family.

"Gloria," I heard our neighbor call over the fence that connected her yard with that of my parents, "could you please do me a favor?" I was sitting in the back yard in a deep state of depression.

"What is it, Sarah?" I answered, almost afraid of what she was going to ask me. It was not a good time for me.

Sarah did not drive and needed a ride to her sisters' for her nephew's birthday. It took us about ten minutes to get to the apartment where they lived. I dropped her off and told her I would be back in about an hour to pick her up. Sarah insisted that I go in with her so I gave in and met the birthday boy. He was not a boy at all, but a very pleasant and good-looking man. His name was John Paris. I took an instant liking to him and was glad that I had come.

The next day Sarah called me at work. She was very excited and confided in me that her nephew had asked for my phone number and was going to call me and ask for a date.

"Now act surprised," she said, "I don't think I was supposed to tell you."

John was a member of a senior drum corps, the Appleknockers, in Geneva, New York. When he called to ask me out it was to accompany him to their annual dinner dance. I told him I would love to go, but I could not dance. He just laughed and said, "Thank goodness, Gloria, neither can I." It was an unbelievably wonderful evening and we dated for months before becoming engaged.

Stephen adored John from the beginning and when I brought him to John's rehearsals he enjoyed running around and pretending that he was a member of the corps.

We were married in St. Patrick's Church with Stephen as the ring bearer. Following our honeymoon in Florida we moved to an apartment in Seneca Falls. John worked for the government at the Seneca Army Depot, a facility used for the storage and maintenance of weapons and other critical materials.

John wanted to adopt Stephen right after we were married, but we had to wait for six months to go to court. At the hearing John became his legal father, and our son was now named Stephen Michael Paris. We celebrated with our parents, relatives and friends at a party, and when John held him up high they were both laughing as everyone cheered.

Our family situation changed dramatically at this time. While my

John and I were married in St. Patrick's Church in 1960.

Aunt Margaret was the only one in the Giovannini family who had tuberculosis, many of my uncles had untimely deaths due to heart problems. Uncle Aldo, whose wife had not survived her brave battle with cancer, had a fatal massive heart attack. He left behind their son, Aldo Giovaninni, Jr., who was just seven years old. My uncle had named my mother as the guardian of his son. We all embraced him, welcomed him into our family, and to Maryann and I he became the brother we never had.

While we were busy making plans to have my uncles Mario and Lee build our new house I discovered that I was pregnant again. We were thrilled and could not wait to share our good news. Our plans to build a house were put on hold.

Our son Gregory John was born at Taylor Brown, a beautiful healthy baby. The hospital administrator had arranged for me to have a private room at no cost, and when our son was born she announced the birth over the hospital's loudspeaker system. John and I were overjoyed. I had a normal delivery once again, and we had an adorable healthy baby boy. As I held my baby for the first time I could not help but wonder what Dr. Severson would have thought. This was truly my second miracle and another one of the happiest moments in my life. One of the first things people noticed about Greg was his extraordinarily long eyelashes. He drew admiring glances everywhere we went. Stephen loved to hold his baby brother and looked forward to the day they could play together.

Our apartment no longer filled our needs so we decided to have my uncles build a house for us. While working on the house, they kept coming up with changes that would be beneficial to me. Basement steps with a rail on each side was one of their innovations. This proved to be of immense help to me as my mobility became more limited. We made a wise decision to have the master bedroom and bathroom on the first floor. Our house was located in the middle of a street that ended in grasslands. It was made up of young families, the majority of which were Italian Americans. Some had been born in Italy and often talked about their beloved homeland. One of the traditions in the neighborhood was to visit the new homeowners and bring home baked goods. There were many children on this street and our front yard was a popular playground. We all looked after each other's children. This was a big help to me as I was unable to run after mine. My dear friend Joan, who lived right across the street, did it for me. Following mass on Sundays you could hear mothers calling their children in for the traditional Sunday pasta dinner. Neighbors spent a lot of time in their gardens growing fresh vegetables and kept their lawns immaculate.

With our children Anne, Steve and Greg in 1967.

I had no problems caring for two children and found it easy to carry Greg around with me wherever I went. Three years later, when our daughter Anne Margaret was born, I was not at all concerned about the dire predictions that had taken place more than ten years before. Once again things went well, and John and I were now parents of an unbelievably beautiful baby girl. Another happy moment — another miracle. When we brought her home we had her two brothers with us in the car. As we pulled into our driveway there were children in the neighborhood lined up on each side of our driveway. They had come to welcome our baby girl — and their future playmate.

Raising our family and making sure that they were the happy children of my dreams, and that they remained healthy, became our top priority. John did not like to talk about his own childhood. It had been very different than mine, but he too had been one of the lost children. Together we tried to do all of the things with our children that we had never done while we were growing up. We went to festivals and fairs, zoos and nature centers, children's museums, amusement and theme parks. Sometimes my parents accompanied us on our family vacations. Biggs had offered constant exposure to the arts, music and theater. Now we did the same with our children. Regardless of what their interests were, we made it a point to be involved and to help in any way that we could.

Stephen was our adventurous one who loved to explore everything and we never knew what he would be up to next. Greg was quiet, an intense child who amazed everyone with his creativeness. Anne was very outgoing and shared the adventurous spirit and creativity of her older brothers. John and I attended school functions, joined the parents' groups, and volunteered as chaperones on class trips.

Making sure that they remained healthy would not have been as much of a challenge if I had not been such a hypochondriac whenever they became ill. A slight fever or cough threw me into a panic, and if they became sick I felt like I had butterflies in my stomach. I could not eat or concentrate on anything until they recuperated. Fortunately for me — and for them — they were very healthy except for the usual childhood illnesses and upper respiratory infections.

"You are making me nervous by asking so many questions," our pediatrician remarked one day in his office after examining one of our children. "Mothers who are health professionals such as yourself are paranoid about your children's health."

Of course he was right. I was afraid that they might have a serious illness, perhaps even tuberculosis. At the request of the Public Health Department they each were required to have a tuberculin test every year for several years. They were always negative, but it took time to finally put this fear behind me.

When our children made their first Communion and confirmation I could not help but reflect back on my own confirmation when I had been asked to sit in a room in back of the altar.

As I watched our children walk up to the alter to receive the sacraments— our daughter wearing a beautiful white dress and veil, and our sons in their Sunday best, I prayed that they would never be exposed to the prejudice and isolation that I had experienced in this same church. Even though I had not yet shared with them the story of my illness, I talked to them about how important it was to help people who were less fortunate than they were. We also talked a lot about discrimination and prejudice and how to deal with it, regardless of whether it was towards them or other people.

Every summer during their vacation they organized a neighborhood carnival as a benefit for victims of muscular dystrophy. One of these victims was a classmate of theirs who spent his days confined to a wheelchair. They spent weeks getting ready for the carnival. Other children in the neighborhood were asked to help and they did so willingly. Weeks before they put up posters advertising the carnival. The carnival took place in our yard and featured games, food, and entertainment. Other parents helped, and John grilled hotdogs on our small porch. When it was over the huge glass jar full of money was proudly carried in and emptied on our kitchen table. Everyone helped to count the money and a check was sent to Jerry Lewis's Annual Telethon. In doing this I felt that they learned an important lesson in life, helping others who were less fortunate than they were.

While raising a family I was not aware of the changes taking place in my mobility. They took place gradually. I never gave it a thought when I found it was easier for me to walk when I was pushing a stroller or a cart in a store. It gave me better balance and I did not get so tired. To compensate for my fatigue when doing housework, cooking, shopping, and caring for my family, I began to get more and more organized. This was a great help when preparing for entertaining, holidays, and other events. I started very early and did just a few things at a time. If I did not do this my back would ache and my left knee would become swollen and was very painful. I started sitting on a kitchen stool while preparing meals. John helped me so much. I do not know how I would have managed without him. Our children learned to do their own laundry and take care of their rooms at a very early age. They never complained — at least not to my knowledge.

At work my left knee seemed to become more and more unstable and began filling with fluid. My orthopedic doctor kept draining fluid out of it, which offered some relief, but it did not last. In a consultation with a knee specialist he wrote that I had "gross shortening of the left leg and fixation of the left hip ... left knee is markedly unstable in all directions ... a deformed knee with thin bone structure and malalignment consistent with ligamentous instability." At work I realized that being on emergency call was becoming more and more difficult. It became so much of a problem that I was referred to a knee specialist. No one had ever really said if there was a relationship between the atrophy of my impaired knee and my tuberculosis or long-term use of casts. This specialist made two recommendations. One was to have the knee fused and the other was to wear a full-length brace. I decided to try the brace, but it was so heavy and limiting that I gave up on it and just started using Ace bandages and elevating my leg whenever I could. When I told him about my difficulty with being on call at the hospital he wrote a letter to the laboratory director stating that I could no longer perform that extra responsibility. He added that as long as I was able to perform my duties in the microbiology section of the laboratory he anticipated that I would be able to continue working without aggravating my symptoms. This also put an extra burden on my co-workers, something I had tried so hard not to do.

I tried to make it up to them by helping them with their workload. Several times a year I entertained them with pool parties and barbeques. Many laboratory celebrations took place in our home.

When my mother opened a dress shop in downtown Seneca Falls she wanted me to help manage the store. After working there a few days I found that it was physically impossible to work in a place where I had to be on my feet most of the time. Instead I helped out by writing the scripts and acting as the mistress of ceremonies at her fashion shows. Occasionally I accompanied her to New York City to purchase merchandise for the store.

It was not only walking or standing for long periods of time that was so trying. Sitting with a fused hip presented additional problems. When sitting in a chair I have always had to sit on the left side with my leg hanging over it — I cannot bend my hip. If I sit in chairs with arms, or in booths, I either have to sit in a slanted position or push myself towards the front of the chair to balance myself. In any situation involving having to sit in a middle seat, such as on an airplane, I am extremely uncomfortable. Lying down is the only position that I am completely comfortable in.

* * *

It all went by so fast and suddenly our children were teenagers — very active teenagers. We were delighted with their achievements. I served on the Seneca Falls District Board of Education and was president of the Seneca Falls Schools Music Boosters. Now that our children were older and involved in their own activities I had more time for various charitable and civic affiliations. While at the time I was enjoying every minute of my active life, things were not going as well for me physically. Walking was becoming more and more difficult and I started hanging on to whoever I was walking with. Sometimes I placed my hand on a wall or piece of furniture to balance myself and avoid falling. One day while I was walking with Greg he said, "Mom, I think a cane would really help you walk better." It was obvious that I was struggling to walk even while holding on to him.

We went into a drugstore and purchased one that very day. Using a cane helped tremendously, but I hated using it because I identified it with being old. On the bright side, it was close to my fortieth birthday, and I was still not wheelchair-bound as my doctor had predicted.

While my children went on to undergraduate and graduate schools, John received several promotions. Life was good. Just before each of our sons got married I asked a friend who had been a professional dancer if she would teach me how to dance. I wanted to be able to do the slow dance traditionally done at weddings with the groom and his mother. We spent hours practicing. This time as I held on to my sons I did not need a cane. By then I had become so used to using a cane that it did not bother me, that is until a few years later when our daughter was to be married. As mother of the bride I would be escorted to the alter by my two sons, and I wanted to look my very best. I did not want to use my cane at the wedding reception. Our good friend Michael, who made all of the exquisite flower arrangements for the wedding, knew that I was having a real problem with this. On the morning of the wedding he attached a special arrangement for my cane that matched the bridesmaids' bouquets. "Look at you," he exclaimed, "you look just like a queen." For that day I felt like one as well.

Today Anne is a doctor of audiology and director of Hearing Evaluation Services of Buffalo, Inc., located in Amherst, Williamsville and Orchard Park. She is married to Joseph Orsene and together they have four sons, Kyle, Giovanni, Luciano and Sebastian. Greg obtained an MBA in finance and information systems from the University of Rochester. He is currently manager of Marketing and Finance Systems for a major retail company headquartered in San Francisco. Steve graduated from Auburn Community College and worked in law enforcement. He is married to Wendy and they have a son, Brandon. We are a close-knit family and make every effort to spend time together and carry on our family traditions.

* * *

My mobility continued to be affected by my disability and soon I had to use two canes. Now, because both hands were not free, I was unable to carry anything. There were frequent falls. When my doctor recommended having physical therapy I discovered that my insurance put a limit on the number of visits. Every few months I had to get another approval. Going to physical therapy became a routine part of my life, as did swimming. There is such a feeling of movement and independence when in the water. Both the therapy and swimming helped tremendously.

As I approached middle age I realized that even the canes were not helping me. It was time to start using crutches, and I am still using them.

At first I was very upset as I felt it was a step back. Would a wheelchair be next?

Walking permanently on crutches was difficult, but I soon realized that they were so much easier to use than the canes. Now I could walk faster, carry things, and feel safer when climbing stairs or dealing with sidewalk curbs. There was less strain on my back. Still, whether I used canes or crutches, I always had to be careful not to put the rubber tips down on things that would cause me to slip and fall. I had found this out at Biggs and was always careful. However, now I was walking in an entirely different environment. It is still frustrating to be constantly looking down to make sure I am not walking on surfaces that are slippery or uneven, wet or icy. Leaves and small pieces of paper (especially cellophane wrappers) can also be treacherous. Every room and all steps in our home are carpeted. There are no throw rugs.

I did try using forearm crutches that are designed for long-term use, but they did not work for me. My crutches were made of aluminum and had to be replaced at least once a year. I usually had more than one pair. When we painted a pair for a Halloween party my family thought they were really "cool," so my husband started painting every pair I owned. One day a very unusual-looking long and narrow package arrived in the mail. Inside I found a black pair of the latest in designer crutches, superior in every way to the ones I had been using. They were much sturdier and came in a variety of colors, with a selection of decorative crutch covers and accessories. Since they were epoxy-coated they did not chip like the ones that were spray painted. Our son Greg had sent them.

When it became impossible for me to use my crutches for more than a short distance I started looking into getting a wheelchair — one that I could keep in our car and use as needed. This turned out to be an excellent idea and actually made me more independent. There have been so many advancements in medical technology, including improvements in wheelchairs. Through the ongoing research of scientists, inventors, and bio-medical engineers, newer products are constantly being introduced. Sometimes it is the person who is or becomes disabled that is responsible for changes. Such is the case of a young woman, Marilyn Hamilton, who became a paraplegic following an accident. She could no longer participate in sports and was impatient with her bulky wheelchair. Marilyn designed an ultra-light sturdy wheelchair which came in "hot" colors that she called "screaming neon chairs," stating, "If you can't stand up, stand out."

Today there are different types of wheelchairs for disabled people

to use in sports. It would have been fun to have one of those when playing wheelchair games at Biggs. In 1980 Marilyn was co-founder of the
Quickie Wheelchair Company. My first wheelchair was the Quickie
"Breezy." It was a flashy brilliant blue and I called it the Glomobile. I
used this lightweight portable wheelchair in traveling with my family.
It has been on ships and airplanes, making it possible for me to visit
places in this country and abroad. There are many fond memories of
these trips. My Glomobile was lowered from a cruise ship to a tender
and then wheeled on the white sands of Caribbean island beaches. In
Rome I bounced up and down on the seat while riding over cobblestone
streets. The Glomobile had a life span of twenty years and was replaced
by Glomobile2. This one could be used as a standard self-propelled
wheelchair or a transport chair. All that was required was to remove the
large wheels.

* * *

While traveling with my family in Florida I noticed people using
power-operated scooters. As I watched them zip around with apparent
ease, I decided to contact my insurance company to find out if our policy would help pay for one as it did for wheelchairs. When I got home
my doctor signed the mandatory certificate of medical necessity and I
sent it in immediately. The insurance company turned down my request
in a letter stating that these scooters were recreational vehicles and not
covered. In my next letter I wrote, "If these are recreational vehicles why
aren't they sold in the sporting goods section of stores? I can only find
them in medical supply stores." They turned my request down again. I
then contacted New York State senator Michael F. Nozzolio. He had an
office in Seneca Falls, and a reputation for getting services for people in
need of medical assistance. Senator Nozzolio contacted the insurance
company. Within a week my request was granted. I chose a compact,
red, three-wheel scooter that ran on batteries. It was easily disassem-
bled and fit into our car trunk. I called it my Harley. My next one was
a bright blue updated version. It was amazing how well this vehicle
moved on the ground outside, even on rough terrain and hilly areas.

I had many interesting experiences with this scooter. When they
were younger, each of our five grandsons loved to sit on my lap and
have a ride. One day John and I went to Hobart College in Geneva, New
York, just a short distance from where we lived. Hilary Clinton, accompanied by her husband, President Clinton, was speaking there. Spectators lined up behind a taped area. Afterwards the Clintons, guarded by

Getting ready to tour the streets of San Francisco in 2000 as a passenger on Greg's motorbike. It sure beats riding in a wheelchair.

secret service men, greeted us. President Clinton saw me in line on my scooter. He leaned down so that we had eye contact and took a moment to speak to me.

The first time I drove downtown on my scooter I stopped to talk to a man I knew who usually went walking there with his wife. When I asked where she was, he told me that she had been having so much trouble with her legs that she could hardly walk. I suggested to him that he might want to get a scooter like mine for her. She could join him when he took his walks. This man just shook his head and said to me, "Oh no. She would be too ashamed." His remark really upset me. Should I be "ashamed" as well? I realized I should not have been surprised by his remark. No one likes using canes, walkers or crutches. To many the use of wheelchairs and other mobility aids is a signal to others that they are sick, helpless, incapable, and weak. They would also rather not hear or see well than resort to visual and hearing aids.

A good example of this took place when President Franklin Delano Roosevelt was in office. From the 1920s through the 1940s people looked at those with disabilities in fear. Many Americans were frightened when they discovered FDR had polio. They wondered how a "cripple" could be president. He was well aware of this and did many things to hide his disability. He was never seen in his wheelchair nor was he lifted from it in public. He always appeared standing up, steadied by an aide, or seated in a regular chair. Of 35,000 photographs taken of him, only two ever appeared of him in a wheelchair. He had the bottoms of his braces painted black so they did not show. Despite his disability this remarkable man was one of the most outstanding presidents in our history.

Reading has always been an important part of my life. In deciding to write my life story I became intrigued with reading the memoirs of people with disabilities. Everyone's story was different, but they all had some things in common. As survivors they all had a positive attitude, made contributions to society, and were role models for both the abled and the disabled. When I read John Hockenberry's memoir, *Moving Violations: War Zones, Wheelchairs and Declarations of Independence,* I was so moved I read it twice. John Hockenberry became a paraplegic as a result of an automobile accident. He has had an amazing career as a journalist covering news all over the world, as a television correspondent (Dateline NBC), and as a radio commentator (National Public Radio and CBS). His numerous awards include four Emmy and three Peabody awards. Mr. Hockenberry is well known as an advocate and spokesman for the rights of the disabled.

I first met him at the Al Sigl Center in Rochester, New York, where his speaking engagement was followed by a book signing. When I brought my book to him to have it signed, I told him that his book had been an inspiration to me and that he was a fantastic role model for those of us with disabilities. Several years later I had a chance to hear him speak in Syracuse, New York. My husband and I had arrived early, and I spotted Mr. Hockenberry in his wheelchair in the back of the room. I wheeled over to where he was sitting and introduced myself to him for the second time. We talked about our experiences in dealing with our disabilities and using a wheelchair.

* * *

When it became necessary to have a hip replacement on my good leg I was upset. It was the second operation on that leg. After years of putting almost all of my weight on this leg, the hip was in terrible shape. My surgeon showed me my x-rays that revealed, as he put it, "bone on bone." There was severe pain when climbing stairs. Recovery was difficult because I had seldom put any weight on my left leg. After several weeks at a rehabilitation center for intensive physical therapy I gradually recuperated. I was able to use my crutches to walk and climb stairs without suffering any pain. On a follow-up visit I asked my surgeon if he could replace the left hip so that it would no longer be fused. He said it was an excellent idea, but would be impossible because the bones in that leg were much too thin.

John and I were in an automobile accident. My left foot was severely injured and required emergency reconstructive surgery. This surgery was also more complicated because of the permanent effects of my tuberculosis. Again I spent a long time at a rehabilitation center. Since my husband had also suffered complications from the accident, we spent the next few months at the home of our daughter and her husband. A hospital bed was put in their family room. Our grandsons were fascinated by the bed that went up and down, and by my various accessories—crutches, walker, wheelchair, and a foot cast that was changed frequently and came in many colors. Their favorite was the one that glowed in the dark. These boys were the best medicine for me and John during our long recuperation.

These last two surgeries were harder on John than me. He visited me every day and was such a help when I returned home. Determined not to let these setbacks toss me into a depression, or to depress others when I talked to them, I put on my happy face and made it a point to use humor when talking about the accident. One head doctor who came to say good-bye to me upon discharge remarked that she hated to see me go because I had been, in her words, "a breath of fresh air." While I was there we had talked about my tuberculosis and several weeks later she asked if I would talk to a visiting group of medical students from the University of Rochester. She wanted me to tell them about my life-long experience with skeletal tuberculosis, a disease which they had little knowledge of. As they entered my room and stood near my bed, notebooks in hand, they seemed mesmerized by my story and asked many questions. Sometimes I made them laugh, and I think it was at that time that I began thinking about writing the story of how tuberculosis had changed my life. One of my roommates, who upset her family every night with her negativity, asked to be moved to another room. Nothing I could say would bring a smile to her face. When I asked the charge nurse why she moved she said, "She told me that you had too many visitors and that you laughed too much." Her daughter came in that night to apologize for her mother's behavior.

In one large hospital I was in for rehabilitation John would wheel me outdoors and to the cafeteria. When going down the long halls it was heartbreaking to see so many young people in wheelchairs and on stretchers, paraplegics and quadriplegics moving along slowly in their power wheelchairs. Some of them would never leave the hospital. How I empathized with them. They were also lost children.

It is not always easy to find the humor in everyday life, but it is a survival tactic for me. I have always been determined not to turn family, friends, medical personnel — and hopefully roommates — away with negativity and complaining. On a number of occasions I have sent my surgeons, either before or after surgery, a humorous letter about them, the operation, or anything else that I thought they would find humor in. One doctor who got his letter after I was discharged called and asked if I would mind if he shared it with his colleagues.

The day after a scheduled surgery I sent the following letter to the director and fellow members of a board we served on. They had sent me a beautiful arrangement of flowers with a card wishing me well prior to the surgery. It had been cancelled.

> After multiple trips to the theater (hospital) to prepare for my grand opening (surgery) I arrived at the designated pre-show time of seven am. I was feeling so confident, all of my important lines memorized. Lines like DNR and YES I HAVE INSURANCE. Following my complete costume change I began feeling strange ... stage fright? Concerned with this news my co-star and leading man (surgeon) arrived in costume with props in place ready ready for Act 1 of the OPENING OF GLORIA. Then the unthinkable happened ... my stage manager (nurse) discovered I had a fever and the show had to be canceled. It has been rescheduled at the same theater. I have been assured I will NOT be replaced in the lead role or drummed out of the actor's union. Just pray my leading man doesn't get sick.

* * *

When John and I retired we found it to be one of the most enjoyable times of our life together. It was one of spending precious time with our children and grandchildren, one of renewing old friendships, and one of having the time to pursue our hobbies and other interests. We celebrated by taking a cruise to the Caribbean Islands, and getting rid of our alarm clocks. When we returned home, we noticed that neighbors who had retired and had more free time were constantly improving their lawns. In an effort to keep up with the Joneses, or in our neighborhood, names with families whose ended in a vowel — Giovannini, Capaldi, and Lorenzetti — we did the same. I loved to tease my dear friend, Dr. Emanuel Li, that he should consider moving to my neighborhood.

* * *

Soon after retiring I went to the nearest Social Security office to apply for my benefits. When I entered the office and stood in front of the desk of a young girl who would be taking care of me, I told her that I knew I would be taking a cut in my benefits since I was retiring early. She just looked at me and said kindheartedly, "But you are disabled. You will get the full amount." At that time I was on crutches, but it had been a long time since I had considered myself disabled.

I have used my retirement as a venue for my passion for art, writing, public speaking and advocacy for minorities. Creativity comes in many forms, and now that I am no longer working I have more time for decorating projects and painting abstract modern art. Like most writers I seldom go anywhere without pen and paper. Essays, poems, and short stories are among the things I like to write. Attending workshops and belonging to writer's groups creates a great outlet for sharing my works with others while learning more about the art of writing.

* * *

According to the Bible, "A merry heart doeth good like a medicine," Proverbs 17:22.

The idea to perform as a comedian came to me while I was on the board of Options for Independence (OFI), an independent living center that provides services and advocacy by and for those with disabilities.

I was instrumental in hiring keynote speakers for our annual conferences who would integrate humor into their presentations. The first one chosen was Dr. Steve Allen, Jr., a practicing physician and son of the famous comedian. After I introduced him we sat together for the luncheon preceding his talk. He noticed my crutches and the first thing he asked me was what the "hardware" was for. Dr. Allen laughed at my humorous but ridiculous response and suggested that we should go on

Schtickin' around

Two local comedians defy the trends

Gloria Paris, of Sackett Street, Seneca Falls, who is permanently on crutches, calls herself the world's oldest sit-down comedian.

Top: An audience favorite when I started performing as a comedienne (on crutches) in 1998 was my Caribbean cruise act. *Bottom:* John disguised my scooter as a Harley Davidson for my 2004 performance for the Sampson navy veterans.

the road together. Everyone enjoyed his performance. He had a wonderful sense of humor, not only in his conversation with me, but with the audience as well. As I listened to him speak I thought to myself *I can do that*— and I have.

My first performance was in the Senior Follies in Seneca Falls, a well-attended variety show held every year as a benefit for our Historical

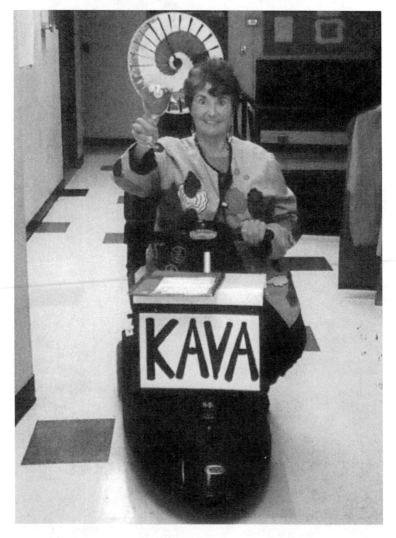

Backstage on my scooter ready to perform as a fun-loving tourist on a Caribbean cruise, enjoying my favorite tropical drink, KAVA, in 2008.

Society. I called myself the world's oldest sit-down comedian. I started performing locally. Most of the material was taken from my own life experiences and from being a senior citizen. Audience favorites included "Is There Life After Fifty?" and "Finding the Humor in Health Care." Local newspapers have written feature articles about me, but the thing that got the most attention was a large front-page colored picture of me wearing a colorful gown and boa while holding a (fake) cigarette on a long holder. (I do not smoke.) I especially enjoyed performing for the annual variety show for the Sampson navy vets. I had met several of them while visiting the Sampson air force Base and Memorial Naval Museum. Both navy and air force veterans established this museum in the original jail (brig) near the entrance of the former base. It was built "to help preserve the park's proud military history." I was overwhelmed with nostalgia when I saw the pictures and artifacts from the largest air force hospital in the nation. We decided to try to find it, but the road ended in a rocky path. Still we went on until we finally saw the rundown abandoned building where I had started my career. It looked like a haunted mansion, surrounded by weeds and covered with foliage we could not identify.

I have always known that there are those who do not expect the disabled to be humorous. It is one of many stereotypes of people with disabilities, along with the myth that disability always equals illness. When I began performing, I was worried that the audience would be so concerned about my crutches— about my disability — that I would lose their attention and gain their sympathy. In order to draw attention away from my disablility I decided to make the crutches a part of my act. With this in mind, I had the house lights to the crutches turned off just before walking out on the stage on crutches. Our son Greg had attached numerous miniature Christmas lights outlining their shape. The entire audience could only see the tiny lights outlining the crutches, and when the lights came on I shouted out some ridiculous reason for why I was using them. My favorite one was, "I should have listened to my grandson when I insisted on borrowing his skateboard." The entire audience forgot about the crutches and the disability. Their enthusiastic response was remarkable as they no longer worried about the crutches or why I needed them.

John is a great help. He paints my crutches in exotic colors, often adding eye-catching props. When I started using a scooter on stage he cleverly disguised it as a Harley Davidson motorcycle, or decorated it with props that fit in with my script. Often audiences who see me after shows are surprised to see that I am still using crutches or a scooter. They actually thought they were part of the show!

When speaking to different groups and organizations I also start with a humorous reference to my crutches. Sometimes there were a few who actually believed my ridiculous explanation. In the middle of my presentation I tell them the real reason I use crutches, and present a brief overview of my life with tuberculosis. Audiences are very receptive to this. So many people have come up to me and said how meaningful it was to them to hear my story. Others share stories with me about members of their families or friends who had tuberculosis or even themselves. They seem to want me to hear their stories and seem relieved to be able to share them with someone. This would never have happened years ago when people avoided talking about the disease. In speaking to the public I try to stress how people with disabilities are becoming more independent, more involved in society, lead more productive lives, and actively contribute to our movement for civil rights for the disabled.

*   *   *

Jim Bero, one of the people that I interviewed for this book, is someone I met through my involvement with our local community theater, the Seneca Community Players (SCP). Jim, a lawyer, ran his family's construction company. When I was asked to serve on the board of SCP I helped produce a show. On opening night I was surprised to see a man being wheeled in on a stretcher. Later I found out that it was Jim, a gifted actor and member of SCP. Jim was recovering from a spinal fusion—a victim of skeletal tuberculosis. He started having problems with his back when he was in his thirties and his doctor told him that in time he would have to have some discs in his spine fused. He sought help from a chiropractor and got some relief, but his agonizing pain and symptoms continued to get worse. The chiropractor felt that there was something else going on and encouraged him to see an orthopedic doctor. Jim went to Strong Memorial, a teaching hospital, in Rochester New York. In order to view his spine a long needle with a miniature camera on the end was inserted. No one expected to find the large mass that was growing there. He was in remission from cancer, and chemotherapy and radiation had left him with a compromised immune system. Doctors assumed that the cancer had spread, but they took a biopsy to confirm this. When it turned out to be negative, the doctors were confused. They could not figure out what was wrong. "In the course of one day," Jim explained, "at least seventy staff members were in and out of my room — medical students, interns, residents, and doctors of various specialties." A doctor who had practiced in Hong Kong was the one who figured it out. He said that he was sure that it was tuberculosis of the spine. Spinal tuberculosis was very common in China, and Jim's appearance, negative biopsy, and x-rays indicated that this was the cause of the mass. A culture taken from the mass proved him right, and a spinal fusion was scheduled immediately. Surgeons made an incision in the front of his stomach. Every bit of the tuberculosis mass was removed. Bone was removed from his pelvic area and placed into his spine to reinforce it. Following surgery Jim was put on a special table, where attendants removed his clothing. He was then literally hung up on thin ropes, and as attendants held onto his arms, legs and head, the entire table — with the exception of a small seat — was lowered. Next he was placed in a body stocking and rolls of gauge dipped in plaster of Paris were rolled around his outstretched body. Once he was returned to his bed an oven shaped like a tunnel was placed over his cast. It took days for it to dry. He could not move as the cast covered him from his neck down to just above his knees.

Jim's experience with tuberculosis took place more than thirty years after mine, but there were many similarities. We both had skeletal tuberculosis and had suffered a lot of pain. Our doctors had a difficult time making a diagnosis and had to rule out the possibility of cancer. Both of us went through the ordeal of a surgical fusion and endured the discomfort of the application of a cast and the long drying process. Neither of us could move following surgery because of the restrictions of our casts. Although we are both cured, we still face the daily ongoing challenges of mobility.

This is where the similarities ended. It had been months after my fusion before I was able to stand up. After just three days a therapist told Jim he was going to help him stand up, but Jim blacked out and had to return to his bed. While I had stayed in the hospital for nearly a year, Jim was discharged in one week. He was given preventative medications for the disease.

Today Jim has much less pain, but has limited movement and stiffness. He has had to adjust to not putting unnecessary stress on his spine, but he keeps active in order to remain as independent as possible. After his discharge he removed a small section of his cast, somehow got into the family van, and had his wife drive him to the construction sites of his business. There, clipboard in hand while in the van, he continued to work.

Jim's story, like so many of the stories of my friends at Biggs, is important to me because it is a story of survival and of not letting his illness define who he is. Our shared experiences have resulted in our becoming advocates for others with disabilities. We try to help those who are not as fortunate as we are. We look at our lives differently than others, perhaps enjoying them more. Our grown children have benefited from our experiences, and we have been fortunate in having loving spouses who do not treat us as different.

*　*　*

Coping with my own disability has greatly influenced my life and my advocacy for minority groups. I have little tolerance for those who discriminate and exhibit prejudice in judging individuals according to their physical and mental abilities, color, ethnic backgrounds, and gender. My strong beliefs in inclusion and tolerance have motivated me in my involvement.

In the late 1960s Independent Living Centers (ILCS) worked towards changing communities to accommodate the needs of the disabled. The movement for disability rights began in the 1970s when accessibility and safety for those with disabilities was a main issue. A powerful coalition of disabled people, along with the help of thousands, led to the passage of the Americans with Disabilities Act (ADA). This civil rights law, signed by President George H. Bush in 1990, was created to assure equal opportunities for the more than fifty million disabled adults and children in the United States. It was the world's first civil rights law for people with disabilities, and hundreds of Independent Living Centers were opened. In the late 1960s these centers were first opened to assist people with disabilities and to encourage them to become a part of the community. Options for Independence (OFI) is one of these centers. I was an officer on its board for many years.

Accessibility to all public accommodations, both interior and exterior, is something I am constantly on the lookout for. This includes handicap parking spaces, ramps, curbs, and aquatic lifts for pools. When CELEBRATE 98 in Seneca Falls was in its planning stages I contacted everyone in charge of this important event. Thousands of people were expected for this celebration being held to commemorate the 150th anniversary of the first Women's Rights Convention held in the village in 1848. A main stage was to be set up for keynote speaker Hilary Rodham Clinton, along with several other dignitaries. I arrived early on my scooter and found thousands of spectators already in front of the stage. No provision had been made for those in wheelchairs and I knew I had to do something quickly. Within a short period of time, with the help of our chief of police and his deputies, an area was cleared and an announcement made for all those in wheelchairs to move to the front. After that incident, with the help of OFI, a checklist for event planners for making their event handicap accessible was issued.

I grew up in an environment of many diverse people who, despite their differences, never demonstrated any signs of discrimination. When I was discharged I became aware of the prejudices and bigotry that seemed to be everywhere. I was deeply troubled. It did not make sense to me but did make me very uncomfortable. I am now an activist for other minority groups who constantly have to deal with it. It is difficult to make a difference, but I have tried to help bring about changes through letters, phone calls, e-mail, and speaking out publicly in the ongoing struggle to provide equal rights for everyone.

When I read about an African American man being dragged on a rope behind a car; or the tragic case of Matthew Shepard, a gay college student who was beaten, tied to a post and left to die, I am devastated. There is no other word for it. I try to keep a close watch on what our government does to prevent hate crimes and what sentences are handed out by the courts where these cases are tried. Following the U.S. Supreme Court's decision (5–4) on June 28, 2000, allowing the Boy Scouts of America (BSA) to exclude gays from its leadership I sent thank you letters to the four justices who had voted against it, and letters of concern and disbelief to the others. I took part in a demonstration regarding this issue that was organized by Dr. Arthur J. Bellinzoni, retired professor emeritus of religion at Wells College (Aurora, New York). He is a biblical scholar, well-known author and speaker, and political activist. Among the people who joined us was the mayor of the city. A man in front of the courthouse yelled obscenities at me as I drove by in my scooter. This was a wake-up call for me, and I made even more of an effort to contact local, state, and federal legislators and ask for help in eliminating the discrimination of our citizens. We are all part of the American family and the political arena.

Whether my feelings are a result of my life experiences I am not sure, but there is one thing that I am sure of. When you are raised in an environment where there is no discrimination, that experience has to play a part in the person you become.

Senator Michael F. Nozzolio at my home after I was awarded the New York State Senate Achievers' Award in 2003.

It is my hope that readers of this book will change their perceptions of those of us who are physically challenged. Sometimes I reflect on what my life might have been like if I had not had tuberculosis.

On May 20, 2003, I was honored as the recipient of the New York State Senate Achiever's Award, given "to acknowledge individuals with disabilities who have risen above those conditions which might otherwise hinder a purposeful life of achievement and fulfillment, demonstrating that the barriers to success for the disabled come more commonly from prevailing attitudes and opportunities than from the physical limitations of a disability." New York State senator Michael F. Nozzolio, an outstanding advocate for the disabled, had nominated me for this award.

Gloria Paris could not be more deserving of the Achiever's Award. She is to be commended for turning her personal challenges into an opportunity to make a difference and help others. It is an absolute privilege to honor Gloria Paris. The strength and courage that she has displayed throughout her life is an inspiration to all of us, and shows that anything is possible through hard work and dedication.

Senator Michael F. Nozzolio

Annual Pilgrimage

Once I was finally discharged and entered college I put the whole sanitarium experience behind me. I never talked about my disability. It was the same throughout my adult life. Although I had undergone a successful surgery after graduating from high school, I still found many things physically tiring and even impossible to do. Still I had to keep trying.

When our three children — Stephen, Greg and Anne — were old enough John and I started taking more family vacations and day trips. One of our favorite places to visit was Ithaca, and we went there every summer. There were so many beautiful parks there that I had visited as a child, and I wanted my family to enjoy them as I had.

Our children were healthy and happily involved in many activities while growing up in our small village. They were the happy children. As I watched them at play I began thinking more and more of my own early years, and of my very different experiences.

Even though they realized that one of my legs was different, and that my mobility was limited, they never asked me questions about it. They were never told about my life growing up in sanitariums, except for an occasional humorous and often exaggerated episode of one of my adventures.

On one summer trip to Ithaca, as we started to pass the entrance to Biggs, I asked my husband to stop the car. For some unknown reason I wanted to tour the grounds and show the campus to my family. As we entered the grounds and drove slowly around the complex I became overwhelmed with memories of the past. They seemed very interested in the buildings, and when we drove to the entrance of the children's building they started asking me many questions. They wanted to know how long I had lived there and what it was like. When I pointed out where my room had been they wanted to know about the other children and where we all went to school.

We parked the car and walked around the building. Everything looked exactly the same as it had when I left, except for one major change. All of the long open porches that encircled the back of the building were now enclosed. It looked so strange to me, and I felt like a piece of my past had been erased. All of the other buildings were intact except for the nurses' residence. It had been torn down. There were signs on the outside of the buildings which identified what sections were being used by state and local agencies.

Our children loved the campus, and as I watched them run around the huge pine trees and up and down the hills I remembered how much I too had loved these grounds. We returned nearly every summer after that and found that there were always changes at the site. My family referred to it as mom's annual pilgrimage.

We stopped making these trips with the children when they got older, although every so often John and I drove there by ourselves to see what changes had been made. Sometimes we just parked the car while I reminisced about my life there.

It was not until years later when our children had left home for college and careers that I found myself constantly thinking about and obsessing over my life at Biggs. Sometimes I spent hours going over again and again in my mind what the inside of the buildings there had looked like. I began searching for and studying all of the old photographs I had. It was time to make another pilgrimage, but this time I needed to go inside of the buildings in order to truly recapture my past. This was when I decided to start putting my story in a journal and to eventually write about it.

We did not bother to check with anyone before we made the trip to Biggs. As we entered the front lobby of the main building we were greeted by a receptionist who wondered why we were there. When I explained to her that I had been a patient there for years and was writing about my experiences she told us that we were free to explore the buildings.

Upon entering the foyer of the children's building I closed my eyes and tried to visualize how everything had looked so many years ago. The once elegant day room had been completely renovated, perhaps more than once. Some areas were partitioned off to make room for offices. There were still a few reminders of the past — a few worn oriental rugs, elegantly framed oil paintings, and an occasional piece of elaborate mahogany furniture. We entered the classroom, now being used as a hospice center, and were greeted by two pleasant elderly ladies. They also were curious about why we were there. When I told them I had been a patient there and that this had been where I attended school, there was a look of amazement on their faces.

"Well," one of them exclaimed, "that explains why these blackboards are on the walls. We never were able to figure that out." Inadvertently I had solved this mystery for them.

We took the elevator upstairs to the second floor, where I showed John the wards and the rooms I had lived in. There was an office in the room I had shared with Jean. Two young men were in there working at their desks. When they asked if they could help us I told them I was revisiting the room I had lived in as a child for more than a year.

"Your desk is right where my bed used to be," I told the man whose desk was the closest to the double window.

Like the women downstairs and others that we ran into on our tour, they had no idea of the history of Biggs Memorial Hospital. I tried to answer the many questions they asked. They had not noticed the plaque with the name Herman M. Biggs on it or realized that this building had originally been a children's building.

Our tour of the main building was equally fascinating. Since this was such a large facility, we decided to just revisit the areas I was familiar with. I remembered that all of the elevators only went to certain floors because the building had been built on different levels. This proved to be a great help to us in locating the places I wanted to revisit. When we entered one of the wards I was surprised to discover that there had been very little renovation. This made it easier for me to point out to John all of the different types of rooms I had lived in. One of them, the end porch, was probably not designed for the purpose of housing patients, but rather as a day room or solarium. When the children's building closed there was a need for more rooms. Using the end porches helped solve this problem, and I spent many months in one of them. There was a window on the wall next to my bed and I was able to open it and visit the children whose room was on the other side. Porch rooms were very bright with windows on three sides and offered a fantastic view of the campus and lake. It was in this very room that on my headphones I first heard the voice of Frank Sinatra. On this pilgrimage, as I entered this room and closed my eyes, I could still hear him sing as young girls screamed in the background.

John wanted to see the diagnostic and treatment areas that he had heard so much about. This included the outpatient clinics, laboratories, and radiology, where I had endured the seemingly endless and frightening trips for repeated testing. Although I knew it would bring back unpleasant memories, I agreed to show him this part of the hospital. All of my memories of being a frightened little girl returned. Memories of lying for hours on the hard x-ray table, of laboratory technicians trying repeatedly to find my tiny veins and inserting tubes through my nose and into my stomach brought tears to my eyes. John sensed that I was getting upset and suggested that it was time to leave that floor and those memories behind.

Main Street had been partially partitioned off, but I was able to recall where most of the rooms had been. How I had loved it there. This whole area was now completely vacant and had apparently been renovated many times. My biggest disappointment was that the auditorium was empty. Even the stage was gone.

After leaving the building we drove around to the back to try to find the opening to the trails and picnic areas where I had spent so many happy days. We were disappointed to find that with the passage of time everything had become overgrown with foliage and we never found the entrance. The only thing left that was familiar was the brook which flowed downhill towards the lake.

It had been a bittersweet experience, and I spent weeks carefully documenting the many changes that had taken place throughout the years.

* * *

Biggs Memorial Hospital closed its doors in 1956. State officials felt that with the success in controlling this disease, and the declining census that resulted, it was time to close this facility. Other sanitariums across the country were also closing.

This decision caused major controversy, especially when state representatives by an overwhelming majority voted to give this five-million-dollar complex as a gift to Tompkins County. It was to be used as a general hospital. Many organizations, including the Patients' Service Committee of Tuberculosis and Public Health Associations, the administration and physicians at Biggs, and the people who lived in the nine-county area using this hospital, felt that it should not be closed. Although it served fewer inpatients, the number of outpatients seen there had increased significantly. Opponents felt that this state-owned property should not be given away as a gift to the county, and that it was not fair for the state government to give away taxpayer property. They felt that other options, such as using it as a state hospital for mental patients, should be investigated. Many people felt that the move to other sanitariums would cause unnecessary hardship to the patients already curing at Biggs.

In the summer of 1956 the transfer of patients began. Under the supervision of the hospital's director, Dr. N. Stanley Lincoln, patients were moved to Mount Morris, Ray Brook, or Onondaga Sanitarium.

It was not long before many changes started taking place on the acres of land that had played such an important part of my life. These changes have been ongoing. First the nurses' residence was demolished to make room for the Cayuga Medical Center. A new 204-bed acute care facility was built. Its modern architecture does not match that of the remaining buildings. For years many different agencies were temporarily located in the Main Building (Biggs A Building) adjacent to the Cayuga Medical Center. In 1997, as the seventy-year-old building continued to deteriorate, the county moved the various services they had there to downtown Ithaca. Also that year the Tompkins County Public Health Department moved its offices to the Children's (H) Building. One of the wings (D-1 and D-2) was the next to be demolished.

In April 2006 the Town of Ithaca Planning Board granted Preliminary and Final Site Plan approval for the proposed demolition of the Biggs A Building. One of the conditions of this was that whenever possible the mature trees on the project site be protected, and that the site would be graded and landscaped as lawn and meadow. My husband and I visited this site six months later and the building was already partly demolished. Even though I knew that this demolition was taking place, I was not prepared for what I saw the following year, or for the profound effect it had on me. What had once been my home, where I had spent most of my childhood, had been reduced to piles of rubble in a vast area of nothingness.

"Oh no," I said to my husband, distraught with what I saw.

A sinking feeling of loss overcame me as we walked over to a huge pile of stones. I carefully picked one up and placed it in my purse. It would stay with me forever. Today I have it on my desk — a paperweight holding down memories of the past.

*   *   *

There had never been an annual pilgrimage or in fact any trip at all to Homer Folks. Not only was it too far away, but I was so young at the time that it had never even occurred to me that I should visit there. As I began gathering more and more material for this memoir, I realized that I really needed to make yet another pilgrimage.

Through researching on the internet I discovered that Homer Folks Hospital had closed in 1973. It was the last of the state's seven tuberculosis sanitariums to close. Closure here was inevitable, just as it had been at Biggs—and for the very same reasons. Still it came as a shock to the community when the announcement was made. There was a concern that the complex would not be used for other things and would be left vacant. Suggestions were offered with the intent of finding additional uses for the complex. This area had few employment opportunities and employees of the hospital worried about finding jobs. They were given the chance to transfer to other state jobs, including state colleges.

Today Homer Folks is used by many agencies and still employs a large number of people. In addition to the Department of Health, the New York State Office of General Services and the Broome County ARC are located there. Some of the property is owned and used by the State University College at Oneonta. Job Corps, a division of the Employment and Training Administration of the United States Department of Labor, houses the Oneonta center in the main building. There are more than one hundred of these centers in the nation.

* * *

While I was doing research on and making plans to visit Homer Folks I received an e-mail from a man who had found my name on a website. I was looking for information about Homer Folks. He told me that while I was a patient at that hospital he had been the oldest of the staff kids. His late father, who became interested in tuberculosis after having been cured himself, was the assistant director there at the time. He remembered that in 1935 Governor Herbert Lehman dedicated the institution on a day when the temperature was 90 degrees. Like my good friends at Biggs, Warren and Daegan, he too had the run of the place. On that day he had joined the other children of staff members watching from the hill overlooking the main hospital building. There were several other e-mails from people who had worked there. One man had worked nights for the Oneonta Job Corps. He had found that late at night he was sure he could feel the presence of those who had died there. It had made him very sad. Others who contacted me sent me e-mail addresses and phone numbers that I could use in my research.

John and I decided to make a trip to Homer Folks. I checked with local government offices in the city of Oneonta to find out what had become of this hospital. The city clerk sent me a letter saying that alderman Julie Carney had read my posting on the city's guestbook. When I contacted her she told me that she had grown up in Oneonta and knew the city well. She kindly offered to help with my research. Julie told me that, according to her research, I had probably been one of the first patients admitted to Homer Folks. John and I wanted to meet Julie and to visit Homer Folks. Arrangements were made to meet her in the city for breakfast and from there to visit both the main and children's building. During the nearly three-hour drive to get there I realized how it must have been for my parents to travel this great distance to visit me.

Oneonta is a beautiful city, the Catskills are glorious, and I could understand why this area had made a perfect site for a sanitarium. We drove to the main building first and I noticed how similar the layout

John and I made a visit to the former Homer Folks sanitarium in 2001. I was amazed to find that many rooms had not been changed since I was a patient there.

Alderman Julie Carnie and I standing on what is left of one of the porches on the children's building at Homer Folks in 2001.

was to that of Biggs. There were long wards that now served as dormitories for the Oneonta Job Corps. It is the largest and most comprehensive residential education and job-training program for at-risk youngsters ages sixteen through twenty-four. It seemed to us an ideal use for this former sanitarium. Due to the open house being held that day there was a lot of activity in the building.

On the drive up the steep hill leading to the children's building I was filled with excitement. Perhaps even more so than when I visited Biggs since I had never made a trip to return there. It looked just as it did in the old photographs that I had. Even the statues of the animals

near the entrance, still standing guard, had remained intact — silent creatures of my past. We walked around the outside so that I could locate
the window of the second-floor room where I was first admitted. It was
from there that I, feeling alone and so sad, had looked down and discovered a group of workers installing a small swimming pool. I remembered how happy I was when they saw me in the window and started
waving and calling up to me. They had called me the little princess. Now
the pool was no longer there, just a visible indented area where it had
been filled in.

When we entered the elevator I was amazed at the ornate gate, brass
rails, and colorful tile floor. It looked like an elevator in a fine hotel. Julie
told me it had never been renovated. As we walked down the halls she
pointed out the beautiful original ceiling lights that had never been
removed. Many of the fixtures were also the originals and typical of the
décor of the 1930s. This building was now being used as a day care center for mentally challenged clients. We stopped to talk to several people
who were working there. Unlike the workers at Biggs, they fully recalled
what had been there previously and seemed to take pleasure in talking
about it. In one room I spotted some interesting photographs of Homer
Folks on the wall. One of the employees, who seemed fascinated by my
recollections of my past there, removed all of them and made copies for
me. On the second floor the wards and nurses' stations had not been
changed. We walked out onto the open porches. Something there looked
different, and then I realized that the rails had been removed. Looking
down from the porch the campus looked just as beautiful as I remembered, except that now the trees were so large that much of the view was
obscured.

We went into the sterile-looking room where my casts had been
applied. This room had held such unpleasant memories—the smell of
wet plaster and the feel of the cold stainless steel support under me. All
that remained in this room were the large sinks that had been used to
prepare the plaster for my casts.

In the single and private rooms the closets contained lowered
shelves so that the children could reach them. John laughed when he
spotted a tiny child-sized replica of a toilet in the main bathroom.

"It looks like the architects who designed this place thought of
everything," he said.

The beautiful wooden shelves that lined the walls of the day room
had not been removed. They no longer held the children's books, games
and toys that we had played with from our beds that were wheeled in

there almost every day. It was from this room on one Christmas Eve that I heard my parents talking in hushed tones as they arrived after driving through a huge snowstorm. I could almost smell the pine of the huge Christmas tree that towered over the brightly wrapped gifts below.

When we left Homer Folks I told John that there would be no more pilgrimages as I had done what I set out to do. Now I had the material

Our family in 2002: five grandsons, from left to right: Sebastian, Giovanni, Luciano, Kyle, and Brandon. John and I (right behind the grandsons), and in the back, Greg, Joe and Anne Orsene, and Steve and Wendy Paris.

A family portrait with Steve, Anne and Greg taken in 2007.

I needed for my memoir, and I was satisfied with everything I had seen in both sanitariums.

*   *   *

Mercy Hospital, the Catholic hospital in Auburn where I was first admitted, was closed in 1977. This was at a time when the trend across the state was to reduce acute care beds.

In order to accommodate the needs of the community, the building was used at that time to provide other types of services, such as cancer and diabetes programs. In the mid–1980s the building was closed. Through a HUD grant the building's interior was gutted, and the one-bedroom Mercy Apartments were built. There were forty apartments for senior citizens, which were opened under the sponsorship of the Sisters of St. Francis. We never did make a pilgrimage there, although we did see the Mercy Apartments.

*   *   *

Although I thought my pilgrimages would somehow bring closure, they never did. There is not a day that goes by that I do not think about them. They have been an important reminder of how I survived my illness, and of how blessed I was to have the loving support of family and friends. I was fortunate to have had the care of incredible medical staffs that brought me through all of it. In this nostalgic look at my life, a life changed forever by tuberculosis, I wrote this poem.

"CHANGES"

Changes in our lives
begin the day we are born,
like the rise and fall of seawater tides.
Ocean waters interconnected.
Cresting when hopes and dreams come true.
Crashing when they do not.

Epilogue

By the 1940s in the United States, after the introduction of pasteurization of milk, skeletal tuberculosis caused by *Mycobacterium bovis* was extremely rare. Today it has been largely eliminated as a public health problem in developed countries.

In 1944, after years of research, a new drug (streptomycin) was introduced. Infectious diseases had been treated with sulfonamides and penicillin prior to this, but they were ineffective against tuberculosis. Streptomycin, called the miracle drug, was a great success in fighting the tubercle bacilli. It was the first lasting cure. With chemotherapy the rates dropped dramatically. People started getting well, were generally not contagious after several weeks, and usually felt better in about a month. The new drug had side effects, especially on the inner ear where balance and hearing could be affected if the drug were given in large doses or taken for too long a period. Still it was felt that the positive results far outweighed these negative effects. It appeared that the battle against this debilitating disease was finally over. As streptomycin-resistant tubercle bacilli emerged during treatments scientists discovered that giving combinations of other anti–TB drugs worked better than using just one.

During the 1950s the number of people with tuberculosis went down 75 percent. Social and economic conditions were improving. There were new drugs introduced. Sanitariums were being closed.

Between the late 1960s and the early 1990s prevention, funding and care of those infected with the disease was neglected. It seemed as though the three-thousand-year struggle with tuberculosis was finally over and that the disease had entirely disappeared. Yet it had not.

"Those who do not remember the past are condemned to repeat it."
— Poet and philosopher George Santayana, 1905,
The Life of Reason.

* * *

In the latter half of the past century in the United States there was a tendency to remain complacent and to neglect problems of control, treatment and solutions when the rates were down.

It was in the mid–1980s that tuberculosis made an alarming comeback. The number of cases in the United States began to rise for the first time in thirty years. There was a 20 percent increase in the number of cases, and an increasing number of the of the deadly MDR TB strains were developing. It was not long before some of the tuberculosis germs began to mutate and become resistant to the new drugs.

MDR TB, multi-drug-resistant tuberculosis, is very dangerous, contagious, and is much harder to treat. It may progress to a potentially lethal stage. There were several factors in this mutation. Patients often failed to complete the full course of drugs necessary to kill all of the bacteria. Sometimes it was because they started feeling better, found taking the drugs inconvenient, or wanted to save money. This allowed the germs to mutate, regroup, and come back armored with drug resistance. Some people, particularly drug addicts, the homeless and the very poor, found it difficult to follow the complicated regimes. Many people, because of the stigma of this disease, refused to get help. A significant deterioration of the infrastructure for TB services was another major factor in this resurgence.

Although it is still true that anyone can get tuberculosis, there are certain groups of people who are at higher risk. Those most at risk are AIDS victims, those such as health-care workers who are often in close contact with people known to be contagious, foreign-born people from countries with high tuberculosis rates, some racial or ethnic minorities, and residents of long-term care facilities such as nursing homes and prisons. Tuberculosis thrives on misery and poverty. Drug addicts, alcoholics, IV drug users, the homeless, and patients who stopped their rather complicated chemotherapy regime are also at high risk. TB is the leading infections killer of people with HIV.

In 1993 cases once again started to decline. There were many reasons for this. Progress was made in improving the chemotherapy regime. There was improvement in the treatment and prevention programs among HIV-infected persons, increased federal government support for state public health infrastructure, and wider screening and therapy for other people considered at high risk. In 2005, although tuberculosis cases were at an all-time low in the United States, progress to eliminate TB was slowing down. According to the CDC there were almost 13,000 cases of tuberculosis in the United States in 2008. However even in upstate New York in the rural community where I live I occasionally read about a case of active tuberculosis being confirmed. There are about 1,800 cases of this disease reported each year in New York State.

Although tuberculosis has been in decline in this country, it continues to remain a major problem globally. After several decades of steadily decreasing incidence, there has been resurgence in many countries. The increasing occurrence of MDR TB, including extensively drug-resistant cases, has resulted in significant challenges to treatment and control worldwide. This is primarily a result of the AIDS pandemic, considering that the human immunodeficiency virus (HIV) specifically affects cellular immunity, which is the first-line defense against tuberculosis.

* * *

Treatment today for people who just have the tubercular infection is to administer preventative therapy. Drugs are prescribed for a certain period to kill the germs that are not doing anything now but may do damage later on. Patients have to undergo periodic checkups. People with active tuberculosis have a demanding regime of four drugs, isoniazid (INH), rifampin (RMP), ethambutol (EMB) and pyrazinamide (PZA), taken daily for six to twelve or eighteen months. Fluoroquinolones, antimicrobial medicines that also kill bacteria or prevent their growth, are also often used. Patients usually just require home care, although in some cases short-term hospitalization might be necessary before they can resume normal life activities. After several weeks a patient can usually return to normal life activities and will not infect others.

Although this disease is no longer contagious after a few weeks of treatment, patients still have to continue taking the prescribed drugs to finish the full course of treatment and kill all of the bacteria. Scientists are continuing to research ways to decrease the number of drugs to take as well as to shorten the length of time necessary for a complete recovery. Surgery to remove a portion of the lung is almost never needed today if the person follows the prescribed drug treatment plan. There are, however, occasions when surgery is indicated to drain pus from wherever it has accumulated and occasionally to correct a deformity of the spine caused by tuberculosis. Musculoskeletal tuberculosis is treated with a different combination of drugs and sometimes surgery is required.

* * *

Prevention of tuberculosis relies on screening programs and vaccinations. More effective vaccines need to be developed. Over the years there have been many changes developed in the Bacillus Calmette-Guerin (BCG) vaccine. This vaccine was no longer effective, and today there are now several strains, making its usefulness limited. It is generally not recommended for use in the United States except for certain people who meet specific criteria, and only in consultation with a tuberculosis expert. In parts of the world where tuberculosis is common, infants may receive this vaccine for prevention of the disease. The TB skin test is used for screening people to find out if they have a TB infection. There is more than one skin test for TB, but the preferred method is the Mantoux test.

In 2009, for the first time, an experimental vaccine was developed that prevents infection with the AIDS virus. Clinical trials have shown evidence that this is a safe and effective preventative vaccine. More research needs to be done before the vaccine becomes available. Since tuberculosis is the leading cause of death among people who are HIV positive, this will have a direct effect on the pandemic of HIV and AIDS. It may eliminate not only the disease but the tuberculosis that is often a result of it. Scientists are also working on a way to deal with the so-called extensively drug-resistant disease, or XDR TB, that renders patients virtually untreatable with available drugs. They have discovered that the combination of two antibiotics (clavulanate and meropenem) have shown positive results in laboratory testing and are currently being planned for patient studies.

* * *

The battle against tuberculosis is not over and the disease remains a public health problem. In the United States the Centers for Disease Control (CDC) is the lead federal government agency for TB prevention, control and elimination. To accomplish this requires a continued effort as well as long-term commitment, new tools, and strong partnerships with other federal health agencies and state and local health departments. This disease is still ravaging much of the world, where it is often out of control. Infectious diseases threaten the economic and political stability of many of the world's nations. Large amounts of suffering and many deaths, particularly in developing nations, demand action on humanitarian grounds alone. Better control and eventual elimination of this disease worldwide will require a strong commitment of the international community.

In 2009 the World Health Organization reported that although the rate of tuberculosis is declining, it is happening too slowly. It is so slow that it would take more than one thousand years to wipe it out. Most of this is the result of a lack of funding, especially in the current global financial crisis. There has been an increase of cases worldwide, including those linked to HIV and MDR TB.

Today there are over sixteen million people with active pulmonary tuberculosis. Out of the eight million new cases reported each year, two to three million will die. It is now estimated that by 2020 there will be one billion cases worldwide, with thirty-five million deaths. Greater action needs to be taken to treat and prevent this disease.

Tuberculosis changes lives, resulting in pain, suffering, and sometimes death. I look forward to the day that it no longer exists.

Bibliography

Books

Beers, Mark H., Robert Porter, and Thomas V. Jones, eds. *The Merck Manual of Medical Information: Home Edition*. Whitehouse Station, NJ: Merck and Company, 2003.

Daniel Thomas M. *Captain of Death*. Rochester, NY: University of Rochester Press, 2000.

Dubos, René, and Jean Dubos, eds. *The White Plague*. New Brunswick, NJ: Rutgers University Press, 1987.

Keith, Lois, ed. *"What Happened to You?" Writing by Disabled Women*. New York: New Press, 1994

McDougal, Gwynn. *The Last Camilles: The Rutland Years 1949–1953*. Sarasota, FL: Acropolis Books, 1995.

Ott, Katherine. *Fevered Lives: Tuberculosis in American Culture since 1870*. Cambridge, MA: Harvard University Press, 1996.

Shapiro, Joseph P. *No Pity: People with Disabilities Forging a New Civil Rights Movement*. New York: Times Books, 1993.

Shaw, Barrett, ed. *The Ragged Edge*. Louisville, KY: Advocado Press, 1994.

Websites

The following websites were used to obtain the facts, FAQs, statistics, and other information on the causes, types, diagnosis, treatment and prevention of tuberculosis. Overviews of tuberculosis today in the United States and worldwide were also used.

www.aafp.org/afp/20051101/1761.htm
www.americanhistory.si.edu/sports/exhibit/removers/wheelchair/index.cfm
www.catskill-gateway.org/medical html
www.cayugamed.org/about/index.cfm
www.cdcinfo@cdc.gov
www.cdc.gov/tb/publications/faqs/qa__glossary.htm
www.ejbjs.org/cgi/content/full/78/2/288 accessed August 17, 2009

www.lung.ca/tb/about tb/forms/bones.html
www.lungUSA.org/diseases/tbfac.html
www.merck.com/mmhe/sec17/ch193a.html
www.merck.com/mrkshared/mmanuel/sec.13c., chapter 157
www.nconnect.net/ — tmsprs/36/scott.html, *Hartford Times-Press*: "This Is No Ordi-
    nary Moment," editorial by Pete Scott, January 26, 1999
wwww.niaid.nih.gov/factsheets/tb.Htm
www.town.ithaca.ny.us/minutes/PB%2004-04-006%web%20min.htm
www.3.niaid.nih.gov/topics/tuberculosis
www.umdng.edu/ntbcweb/tbhistory.htm/Tb history
ww.who.int/mediacentrel/factsheets/fs 104/en/index.html
www.who.int/tb/WHO/Tuberculosis
www.wikipedia.org/wiki/John_Hockenberry
www.wickipedia.org/wiki/Mycobacterium_Bovis

Archive

At the DeWitt Historical Society in Ithaca, New York, I obtained access to the Biggs Hospital Collection. This collection includes newsletters, minutes, correspondence, press releases, and newspaper clippings regarding the Hermann M. Biggs Memorial Hospital, from the years 1949 to 1957. Much of this material has to do with the closing of the hospital in 1956.

Index